Irish Country House Cooking

Irish Country House Cooking

DEIRDRE McQUILLAN

CRESCENT BOOKS
NEW YORK · AVENEL, NEW JERSEY

This 1994 edition published by Crescent Books, distributed by Outlet Book Company, Inc.,
a Random House Company, 40 Engelhard Avenue, Avenel, New Jersey 07001.

Random House
New York • Toronto • London • Sydney • Auckland

ISBN 0–517–10245–5

Editorial Consultant: Roberta Reeners
Index compiled by Helen Litton
Designed by Design Image, Dublin, Ireland
Colour separations by Ultragraphics Ltd, Dublin, Ireland
Printed and bound in Great Britain by
Butler & Tanner Ltd, Frome and London

Photographs
Altamont, Lucy Johnston
Ashbrook, Chris Hill
Ballintubbert House, Derry Moore
Ballynacourty, Davison & Associates
Bermingham House, Seamus Murphy
Carrigglas Manor, Brian Lynch
Cleggan Lodge, Kari Haavisto
Clohamon House, George Gossip
Clonmannon, Bill Doyle
Cuffsborough House, Bill Doyle
Drenagh, Chris Hill
Drimcong House, Mike Bunn
Dysert, Lucy Johnston
Gubbeen House, Barry Murphy
Hilton Park, George Gossip
Kinoith House, Mike Bunn
Luggala, Ken Kirkwood
Mount Falcon, Mike Bunn
Newbay Country House, Brian Lynch
Oranmore Castle, Denis Mortell and Image Magazine
Shanagarry, Lucy Johnston
Strokestown Park House, Ritchie Smith
Tullanisk, George Gossip

All other photographs supplied courtesy of the contributors.

For Paul, Fintan and Tom and in memory of Madge Cleary 1893–1976

♣

CONTENTS

* *Indicates a house which is open to the public or which takes guests. In the case of Altamont and Birr Castle, the houses are private.*

INTRODUCTION

My earliest memories of good food come from the country. As a child, I was sent to stay with my grand-aunts in Tipperary during the summer holidays, and I vividly remember that my shy, gentle aunt, a brilliant cook, was never more at ease than when she was bustling around the kitchen preparing good things for us to eat. There, in her world of scrubbed tables, wooden food presses and the big Rayburn range, she transformed eggs, sugar, butter and flour into endless childish delights – iced chocolate cakes, feather-light sponge cakes, 'patty' cakes, Swiss rolls, madeiras and breads that were devoured as readily as they were made. Her Sunday lunches were unforgettable.

At the end of October every year, my aunt would send a stuffed goose to us in Dublin; at Christmas time, the annual parcel from 'Tipp' contained a turkey, a Christmas cake, tea and other presents. Like many city people with rural relations, we associated the country with the finest and freshest foodstuffs, with flavours and tastes which made lasting impressions.

This book is a celebration of Irish country house cooking, with recipes gathered from houses north and south known for their hospitality and culinary excellence. Some of the recipes have been in families for generations, while others show the influences of contemporary and foreign trends, but all of them make the most of home-grown, wild or local ingredients. Ireland is rich in its raw materials – its incomparable seafood, its fine lamb, pork, beef and game, not to mention its butter, cream and other dairy products. So if a country's table is a mark of its heritage, we in Ireland have a tradition to be proud of, as the sheer variety and scope of these recipes amply prove.

In the 1860s, it was a certain Mr Carden who was the first to open his country house, Barnane, at Templemore in County Tipperary, to paying guests. Today, more and more owners of houses that are architecturally or historically important are finding new ways of earning an income by selling what they do naturally – providing a warm and individual welcome, comfortable accommodation and fresh home cooking. The houses in this book are divided equally among those which are private and those which are open to the public.

Ireland's hospitality has been well chronicled over the decades and visitors have always been struck by its scale and spontaneity. One seventeenth-century observer described the Irish as being 'addicted to hospitality'. The poet Haicéad, in a lament for Eamon MacPiarais Buitléir in 1640 which described his drinking and feasting parties, stated that the man was 'never, never mean with spices', the ultimate accolade at the time.

Substantial breakfasts, a mark of an agricultural society, are still a legacy of Irish country life, reminders of a time when much of the day was spent out of doors. Today, tourists may stare in astonishment at the sheer size of the traditional Irish breakfast – it can consist of porridge (consumption of which goes back to ancient times), black and white puddings (a kind of blood sausage), rashers (healthy-sized slices of bacon) and vast quantities of tea. It is not surprising that this book also offers many recipes for bread and potatoes, some of which can serve as hearty breakfast fare – from Grange Lodge's apple potato cakes, Strokestown Park's potato pudding, an eighteenth-century dish made with potatoes and eggs, to Hilton Park's more contemporary potato brioche with ginger.

Contributors were invited to submit recipes which best reflected their home cooking and, surprisingly, none overlapped. There are excellent recipes for lamb, salmon, pheasant, venison and pork from houses by the sea, by clear Irish lakes, or in the rugged mountains. There are also some very tempting ones for pike, a fish much prized by the rest of Europe but largely ignored in Ireland. For instance, Belle Isle's stir-fry pike with ginger is guaranteed to convert even the most avowed fish-hater, according to Mary Mulholland. There are simple recipes like Altamont's very old one for trout in paper (originally newspaper!) and for pork chops which are glazed in Busherstown House using a butane blow torch. Then there are the more artful and elaborate ones such as Tullanisk's outstandingly good chicken with morels.

Cooking is an art, and there has been something of a culinary renaissance in Ireland in recent years which has a great deal to do with a new-found confidence. Twenty years ago, Rosie Tinne's *Irish Countryhouse Cooking* aimed to improve Ireland's gastronomic image by proving that there was more to it than boiled potatoes and stew. Since that time, no one has done more to promote high standards in Irish cuisine than Myrtle Allen of Ballymaloe in County Cork.

Myrtle Allen opened her Yeats Restaurant in 1964 and a few years later, provided a couple of rooms for overnight accommodation. Today, three decades later, Ballymaloe is rightly included in many guide books. It has thirty guest rooms and a matchless international reputation earned by the freshness of its produce and the simplicity of its cooking. It is represented here by Darina Allen who spreads the culinary gospel according to her mother-in-law through her school at Kinoith. There are others well celebrated, too, like the much lauded Mary Bowe whose haute cuisine at Marlfield House in Gorey, County Wexford (where I spent my honeymoon), is also of world-class standard.

As I want this to be a working cookbook, all thumb marks and stained pages, every recipe has been tested. My gratitude goes to those who helped in this task; to Matt Dowling, Chef Instructor and his students at CERT (The State Tourism Training Agency) who generously agreed to check those from hotels; to Prue Rudd, Alwyn Gillespie, Kate Finnigan, Carolyn McGrath and Geraldine Mitchell; and most particularly to Neil Middleton and Paul Gillespie.

My thanks must also go to my editor, Eveleen Coyle, long-standing friend turned professional accomplice whose idea this was in the first place, and to her assistant Monica McInerney; to Roberta Reeners for her eagle-eyed and rigorous copy-editing; to Deirdre Rennison Kunz of Gill & Macmillan for her superb co-ordination; to Stephen Caviston of Glasthule for his help in locating many out-of-season ingredients; to John Colclough of Hidden Ireland and to Hugh O'Neill whose assistance at all times was invaluable. To all of them, to my contributors and to everyone who uses this book, I hope it gives as much pleasure at their tables as it has given at mine.

Deirdre McQuillan
Dublin, May 1994

Houses & Recipes

All recipes serve four, unless otherwise specified.

♣

With its immensely thick walls, arrow slits and granite floors, Altamont can trace its history back to the 1500s. At one period, it is reputed to have been a convent. The St George family built the main house in the 1700s and also laid out the gardens. During the Great Famine of the 1840s, a lake was dug out to give employment and walks were made through the ancient oak woods of the ice age glen. The present owner, Mrs Corona North, was born at Altamont and has devoted her life to what she calls her 'magic garden'. She runs residential gardening courses, and many of the dishes that she serves are traditional Altamont recipes, often including fish caught in the nearby River Slaney.

Trout in Paper

♣

No one has improved upon the traditional Irish gillies' method of cooking fresh trout. These old fishing guides would clean the fish, dot it with a knob of butter and then wrap it in several sheets of wet newspaper. They would then thrust it into the ashes of a wood fire until the paper started to smoulder.

If such luxuries as a trout-filled Irish lough and a newspaper are not to hand, however, you can use greaseproof/waxed paper and an ordinary oven. Lightly rub the cleaned and gutted fish with seasoned flour. Put a knob of butter, a sprig of parsley and a little thyme or fennel in their insides. Butter a sheet of greaseproof/waxed paper and wrap each fish tightly. Bake in a moderately hot oven (200°C/400°F/gas 6) for 20 minutes. Unwrap at table because the smell upon opening is such a joy.

SPICED BEEF

This traditional Irish dish is served cold on the day after Christmas –
St Stephen's Day – but is just as good all year round.

900 g/2 lb silverside of beef/US bottom round of beef
coarse salt
115 g/¼ lb/½ cup brown sugar
30 g/1 oz/1 US tbsp saltpetre
3 tsp/3¾ US tsp mixed spices (cinnamon, cloves, ginger, nutmeg)

Cover the beef thickly with coarse salt, rub it well in and leave for 24 hours.
Mix the brown sugar, saltpetre and mixed spices with a little more salt and
rub well in again. Leave the meat in this brine, turning it every day for
10-14 days. Then remove the meat from the dish and scrape it clean. Place it
in a large pot and cover with water. Bring to the boil very slowly and
simmer gently until tender, about 3 hours. Allow to cool, then remove and
press it into a round tin or pottery bowl. Cover with a weight to flatten and
put in the fridge. Serve cold and thinly sliced.

MEDLAR JELLY

This is an old family recipe for this strange fruit which first became popular in Tudor times. The medlar looks like a little brown apple but is actually related to the pear family and is eaten when 'bletted' or half rotted. Our own medlar tree is over 150 years old and is usually covered with fruit every year. A very decorative small tree with pretty white flowers in spring and beautiful autumn colouring, it deserves to be more widely grown. It can be bought in specialist nurseries such as ours.

900 g/3 lb medlars
450 g/1 lb sugar to 600 ml/1 pint juice
1-2 lemons, juice and rind

Wait until fruit is soft but skin unbroken, usually in November after a frost. Wash fruit, put it in a preserving pan and cover with water. Bring to the boil, then simmer very gently until it is soft and pulpy. Then strain juice through a jelly bag, preferably overnight. Measure liquid, return to the pan and bring to the boil for 5 minutes. Then add lemon juice, lemon pieces and warmed sugar. Stir until the sugar has completely dissolved. Remove lemon pieces and boil rapidly until jelly sets. The jelly should be a lovely clear amber colour with a wonderful aroma and unique, delicate taste.

'When I first saw Ardnamona from the lake on a beautiful August evening, I felt as if it belonged to a dream world.' Thus wrote Violet Trench in *The Wrays of Donegal*, describing one of the loveliest rural estates in Ireland. Situated on the shore of Lough Eske six miles from the Atlantic, the house was built in 1790 by the Brooke family and was leased to the Wrays, their cousins, who lived there until 1870. Its Edwardian additions were built on by Sir Arthur Wallace when it was his holiday home. The gardens at Ardnamona are internationally renowned for their display of Himalayan rhododendrons and azaleas. Many of these are over a century old, their seeds brought to Ireland from the Imperial Court of China and Nepal.

ARDNAMONA · LOUGH ESKE · DONEGAL
Tel. 073–22650

BAKED SALMON WITH SORREL OR CHIVE SAUCE

4 fillets of fresh salmon
butter
½ glass dry white wine
½ glass water
bay leaf
salt and pepper
beurre manié*
250 ml/½ pint/1 cup fresh cream
good handful of fresh sorrel or chives, finely chopped

Generously smear a flat baking dish with butter. Put in the salmon fillets, then the wine, water, bay leaf and seasoning. Bake in a moderate oven (180°C/350°F/gas 4) for 15 minutes, until cooked. Pour a little of the juice into a pan. Add a knob of *beurre manié* and stir until the juice thickens. Blend in the cream, add the sorrel or chives. Heat through and serve with the salmon.

*Beurre manié: equal quantities of butter and flour mixed together with a fork; small knobs of this kneaded mixture are added to thicken sauces or stews.

Arabel Clarke

RAMSON* SALAD

1 head crisp lettuce
8 rashers/slices streaky bacon
2 ripe avocados, peeled
3-4 ramson leaves, to taste
vinaigrette dressing made with walnut oil and sherry vinegar

Rinse, dry and shred the lettuce and place in a large bowl. Grill the bacon, cool and chop roughly. Chop the avocado flesh. Finely chop the ramson leaves. Add all the ingredients together, add the dressing and toss lightly. Served with chunks of freshly-made bread and butter, this makes a good light lunch or starter.

* wild garlic

CHOCOLATE AND ORANGE MOUSSE

225 g/½ lb/1¼ cups (8 blocks) dark, bitter chocolate
juice and grated rind of 1 or 2 (if small) oranges
115 g/4 oz/1 stick butter
4 large eggs, separated

Melt the chocolate over a gentle heat in the orange juice and grated orange
rind. Then gradually beat in the butter until the mixture is glossy. Beat in
the egg yolks one at a time. Whisk the egg whites separately until white and
firm. Fold the slightly cooled chocolate mixture into the egg whites until
well blended. Leave to sit in the freezer for 2 or 3 hours. It is delicious
served very cold from the freezer, almost like ice cream.

Dating back to the seventeenth century, Ashbrook is said to be one of the oldest houses in Northern Ireland. It has always been owned by the same family, although little remains of the original house built by General Sir Thomas Ash. The elegant bow-fronted entrance with its dressed stone windows and the stable yard were added a hundred years later, as was the spacious dining room with its large Georgian windows.

ASHBROOK.

Co. LONDONDERRY

EGGS ON GARLIC TOAST

This is a rich and delicious first course. It may look complicated but it is,
in fact, very easy.

6 large shallots, coarsely chopped
55 g/2 oz/½ stick butter
4 slices fat bacon, chopped
1 clove garlic, crushed
55 g/2 oz/4 US tbsp flour
570 ml/1 pint/2½ cups Burgundy
340 ml/12 fl oz/1½ cups chicken stock
1 bouquet garni
4 slices white bread
4 eggs

♣

In a heavy saucepan, fry the shallots in the butter for 3 minutes. Then add
the bacon and 1 clove crushed garlic and cook for a further 3 minutes. Take
off the heat and sift in the flour. Return to heat and cook for about
4 minutes, stirring all the time. Add the wine and stock, still stirring, and the
bouquet garni. Simmer with the lid on for at least 1 hour. Pass the sauce
through a sieve and keep hot.

Trim and toast 4 slices bread. Rub with more garlic and put into heated
soup bowls. Keep hot.

Lightly poach the eggs and put on top of the toast. Pour the sauce over
the eggs and serve at once.

A. Beresford Ash

John Beresford Ash.

RACK OF LAMB WITH GREEN PEPPERCORNS

1 rack of lamb of 8 cutlets, trimmed and oven-ready (Keep all trimmings)
butter
4-5 soupspoons/8-10 US tbsp chicken or beef stock
salt and pepper
40 g/1¼ oz/4 tbsp green peppercorns
1 soupspoon/2 US tbsp chopped parsley
strong mustard
2 egg whites

Put lamb and trimmings in a roasting pan in pre-heated oven (maximum temperature 240°C/475°F/gas 9) and roast for 20-30 minutes with a little butter, basting from time to time. Remove meat, strain off juice and keep the lamb warm. Put all juices and trimmings back in the roasting pan with about 4 or 5 soupspoons (8-10 US tbsp) of stock. Season with salt and pepper. Strain again. Pour juices into sauceboat and keep warm.

While the meat is cooking, crush the green peppercorns with the strong mustard and chopped parsley. Beat the egg whites until very stiff, then mix everything together. Heat the grill/broiler to maximum, spread the peppercorn mixture ½"/2¼ cm thick on fatty side of lamb. Grill/broil for 3-4 minutes until nicely coloured. Serve at once.

DARIOLES OF SPINACH

2 eggs
125 ml/4 fl oz/½ cup cream
125 ml/4 fl oz/½ cup milk
salt and pepper
grated nutmeg
30 g/1 oz/2 US tbsp (¼ stick) butter
100 g/4 oz spinach, cooked

Break the eggs into a bowl and whisk lightly. Add the cream and milk, salt, pepper and grated nutmeg. Mix well. Melt about ⅔ of the butter in a frying pan. Throw in the cooled spinach leaves and mix well for 5 minutes. Add spinach to the egg-milk-cream mixture. Melt the remaining butter. With a pastry brush, spread it thoroughly in 4 ramekin dishes and divide mixture between them. Place the ramekins in a shallow ovenproof dish. Fill with cold water about ¾ up the ramekins. Cook in a warm oven (180°C/350°F/gas 4) for 30-45 minutes. When cooked, remove and turn out each dariole onto a plate.

TIAN OF COURGETTES AND TOMATOES

Excellent with rack of lamb.

300 g/10 oz onions, peeled and finely sliced
800 g/1¾ lb tomatoes, ripe but firm
600 g/1¼ lb courgettes/zucchini
2 cloves garlic
olive oil
thyme
salt and pepper

Pre-heat oven to 230°C/450°F/gas 8. Slice the onions finely and cook slowly in a little olive oil, stirring occasionally. Don't brown. Keep warm when done. Slice the courgettes/zucchini and tomatoes finely (5 mm/¼" slices). Rub an ovenproof dish (20 cm/8") copiously with garlic. Spread the cooked onion in the dish and season with salt and pepper. On this bed of onions, lay slices of courgettes/zucchini and tomatoes to produce alternate red and green layers. Season again. Sprinkle with a spoonful of thyme and add 4 soupspoons/8 tbsp of olive oil. Place in pre-heated oven and cook for 30 minutes, pressing down occasionally with back of a slotted spoon.

BLACKCURRANT SORBET WITH RASPBERRY MOUSSE

250 g/8 oz blackcurrants (fresh or frozen)
250 g/8 oz raspberries, puréed
200 g/7 oz/1¼ cups icing/confectionery sugar
300 ml/10 fl oz/1¼ cups cream

to decorate: *blackcurrants with stems and leaves*

Remove stalks and leaves from blackcurrants. Put in blender and process with half of the sugar. Sieve/strain and put in the freezer. Process raspberries and the remaining sugar in a blender. Then put through the sieve/strainer. Beat cream until stiff and mix with the raspberry purée. Serve in deep plates, with 2 or 3 scoops of blackcurrant sorbet surrounded with raspberry mousse.

To decorate, put the remaining blackcurrants in cold water and then dip in caster/granulated sugar. Put one on each plate. A little home-made meringue goes very well with this delicious pudding.

Standing on the site of a medieval stronghold, Ballinlough Castle was built in 1618
and has been in the continuous possession of the same family since that time.
Reconstructed in the 1730s to look like a classic house of the period, it has narrow
windows and a battlemented roof with round corner towers. According to one
nineteenth-century observer, the prospect of the castle was so impressive that it was
'calculated to infuse into the heart of the beholder a mixed sentiment of veneration
and delight'. Major events of the year at Ballinlough include the horse trials held at
the end of August.

SIR JOHN NUGENT BART

BALLINLOUGH CASTLE,
CLONMELLON,
NAVAN,
CO. MEATH,
IRELAND

GRANIA'S SOUP

Excellent for helpers at horse trials or, as we use it here at Ballinlough, for
the mid-morning shooting break.

3 large onions, chopped
8 rashers/slices of bacon (rinds removed), chopped
175 g/6 oz tin of red peppers, drained
800 g/1¼ lb tin of tomatoes, including juice
1.2 L/2 pints/4 cups well-flavoured chicken stock
300 ml/10 oz/1¼ cups single cream or natural yogurt
salt and black pepper

to garnish: *chopped parsley*

♣

Fry the chopped onion and bacon together, adding a little oil if necessary.
Chop the red peppers and add to the bacon and onions. Then add the
tomatoes, including their juice, and the stock. Season to taste. Simmer until
cooked. Liquidise in a blender. Reheat and serve with either a blob of
cream or natural yogurt. Garnish with chopped parsley.

PLUM MOUSSE

We have a very large, old plum tree in the garden and this seems to be one of the best ways of using the fruit.

500 g/18 oz plums
4 rounded tbsp/5 US tbsp granulated sugar
2 sherry glasses of port
1 level tbsp/1¼ US tbsp gelatine
3 eggs, separated
125 g/4 oz/½ cup caster sugar
150 ml/5 oz/⅔ cup double cream, whipped

Place the plums and granulated sugar in a heavy-based pan and cover. Cook over a low heat. As the plums begin to cook, their juices will start to run. Cook until they begin to fall apart, then remove from heat and allow to cool. Remove the stones – a bit of a bore but well worth the effort! Purée the stoned plums and the port in a blender. Sieve/strain the purée to remove the skins and coarse fibres.

Put 4 tbsp/5 US tbsp of cold water in a small saucepan and sprinkle in the gelatine. Leave to soften, then heat gently until the gelatine is fully dissolved. Leave the liquid to cool.

Beat the egg yolks, gradually adding the caster sugar until the mixture is thick and very pale in colour. Fold in the cooled plum-and-port purée.

Whisk the egg whites until stiff. Stir the dissolved gelatine into the plum mixture, then fold in the whipped cream. Lastly fold in the stiff egg whites. Pour the mousse into a pretty glass or china serving dish and chill until set.

APPLE CRISPIE

This humble recipe which can be whipped up at the drop of a hat always seems to go down well.

450 g/1 lb cooking apples
sugar (brown or white)
85 g/3 oz/¾ stick butter, melted
6 tbsp/7½ US tbsp golden/Karo syrup
170 g/6 oz/1½ cups cornflakes

Peel, slice and gently stew the apples with a little sugar and a tablespoon or so of water. Do not oversweeten the fruit while stewing. When cooked, place in a pie or soufflé dish.

Melt the butter in a saucepan. Then add the syrup and stir until blended. Mix in the cornflakes. Spoon this mixture over the stewed apple (overfill the dish, as the cornflake mixture shrinks during the cooking). Place in moderate oven (180°C/350°F/gas 4) for approximately 10 minutes. Watch it carefully, as the top burns easily.

Ballintubbert House is a classic eighteenth-century Irish glebe house owned by the actor John Hurt and his wife Jo. The British poet laureate, Cecil Day-Lewis, was born here in 1904. Three storeys at the front with a two-storey Victorian addition at the back, the house was recently restored by the designer Anne Millais. It is now an established tradition that everyone who comes to stay there cooks at least one meal during their visit and leaves a recipe in the visitors' book.

BALLINTUBBERT HOUSE, ATHY, CO. KILDARE, EIRE.

SMOKED MACKEREL PÂTÉ

225 g/8 oz smoked mackerel fillets (remove skin)
170 g/6 oz/¾ cup cream cheese
juice of ½ lemon
ground black pepper
pinch of cayenne pepper

to serve: *lemon wedges, brown toast and salad*

♣

Set aside half of one of the mackerel fillets. Put everything else in a food processor and whiz until reasonably smooth and well mixed. Drop the remaining piece of mackerel in the processor and whiz it around momentarily so that some larger bits mix in with the pâté. Serve with lemon wedges, brown toast and salad.

BALLINTUBBERT BROWN BREAD

Makes 2 loaves.

This recipe makes a nice crusty, yeasty loaf. It is also excellent for pizza crusts (do not let it rise a second time) and dinner rolls.

225 g/½ lb/2 cups strong white (unbleached) flour
225 g/½ lb/2 cups strong wholemeal flour
225 g/½ lb/2 cups malted brown granary flour
455 ml/16 oz/2 cups water, warmed to blood heat (40°C/100°F)
1 tbsp/1¼ US tbsp brown sugar
1 tbsp/1¼ US tbsp active dry yeast
1 tbsp/1¼ US tbsp salt
olive oil and white flour to coat

♣

Mix the three flours together in a large bowl and put somewhere warm. Add sugar to water and mix to dissolve. Add yeast to the sugar-water, mix to dissolve and wait until it has a foamy, yeasty head. Now add the salt to this mixture, stir to dissolve and pour the whole lot over the warmed flour. Mix briefly with a large wooden spoon and turn the whole mess out onto a large board. Mix it with your hands and knead until smooth and elastic, adding a small amount of flour if necessary to keep it from becoming too sticky. Knead the dough into a ball and coat liberally with olive oil. Put the dough back into the large bowl, cover with a clean tea towel/dish cloth and leave it somewhere warm and draught-free for 1-1½ hours until doubled in bulk.

When the dough has risen to about twice its volume, punch it down and form it into two plaited/braided loaves. Put each loaf into a loaf tin coated with olive oil and sprinkle the top liberally with white flour. Leave to rise for an hour or so in a warm place as before. When risen, put the loaves into a hot oven (200-250°C/400-500°F/gas 6-10) on a baking sheet (or onto the floor of the roasting oven of your Aga) and bake for 30-40 minutes until well browned – it should pull away from sides of tin and sound hollow when tapped. Remove from tins when you can handle them without burning yourself. Leave to cool on wire racks.

SUMMER PUDDING

4-5 slices white bread, crusts removed
115 g/4 oz/½ cup redcurrants
115 g/4 oz/½ cup blackcurrants
500 g/18 oz/3 cups mixed summer fruits, including gooseberries, rhubarb,
raspberries, strawberries, blackberries etc. (cut rhubarb and strawberries
into smaller pieces)
115 g/4 oz/½ cup granulated sugar
3 tbsp/3¾ US tbsp water
1 cinnamon stick
1 piece orange zest
1 piece peeled ginger (1¼ cm x 1½ cm/½" x ½")
1 tbsp/1¼ US tbsp Grand Marnier

to decorate: *mint leaves and whole raspberries*

to serve: *whipped cream*

♣

Line a pudding basin/glass bowl with triangles of bread, leaving aside some to form a middle layer and a top. Put all of the fruit, except for the strawberries and raspberries, into a pan with the sugar, water, cinnamon stick, orange zest and ginger. Bring to the boil, then simmer for between 20-30 minutes until almost tender. Remove from heat, add raspberries, strawberries and Grand Marnier. Cool for 15 minutes, then remove the cinnamon, ginger and zest.

Pour half of the fruit mixture over the bread in the pudding basin. Put another layer of bread over this. Use a slotted spoon to put the rest of the fruit into the basin. Pour on half of the remaining juice. Place the last triangles of bread on top. Place a saucer on top of the pudding, pressing down a little to bring the juices to the top. Then put a weight on the saucer. Leave to cool and then refrigerate overnight. Turn out onto a plate. Patch up any bits of bread that are still white with the remaining juices.

Decorate with mint leaves and raspberries and serve with heaps of whipped cream.

When Irish antiquarian George Stacpoole and his Italian wife, Michelina, a knitwear designer, bought Ballynacourty in West Limerick in 1963 with ten acres of land, it was a derelict building. Over the years, together with local builder Stephen Clancy, they have transformed it into a comfortable family home and converted two fields into a two-acre garden. As a result, the house now looks as though it has been part of the landscape for generations. Ballynacourty is noted as much for its impressive variety of antiques as it·is for Michelina's superb home-cooking.

BALLYNACOURTY,
BALLYSTEEN,
ASKEATON,
CO. LIMERICK.

CURRIED PRAWN SALAD

225 g/½ lb peeled prawns/shrimp
115 ml/¼ pint/½ cup home-made mayonnaise
1 tsp/1¼ US tsp curry powder
1 tbsp/1¼ US tbsp tomato chutney
2 drops tabasco sauce
1 head lettuce
1 lemon, cut in wedges

to serve: *brown bread*

♣

Blend the curry powder with the mayonnaise. Mix in the tomato chutney
and tabasco sauce. Wash and drain the lettuce and arrange on a serving
dish. Place the prawns on top of it and pour over the mayonnaise. Place
lemon wedges all round and serve with brown bread.

*Michelina
Stecpoole*

Cannelloni Ripieni
with Mushrooms and Limerick Ham

Being Italian, my friends always expect a hint of Italy, so this recipe is a mixture of Irish and Italian.

To prepare the pasta
450 g/1 lb/4 cups flour
1 level tsp/1¼ US tsp salt
3 eggs, well beaten
4-5 tbsp/5-6 US tbsp cold water

Sift flour and salt into a large mixing bowl. Make a well in the centre and pour in the beaten eggs. Add some water and mix well with your fingers until the pasta dough is just soft. Sprinkle a large pastry board with flour and knead the dough on it with the flat of your hand until the dough is smooth and elastic, about 10-15 minutes. Divide dough into four equal parts. Using a rolling pin, roll out one piece at a time into a paper-thin sheet. Sprinkle with flour, fold over and repeat the process with each piece. Leave to rest for 15-20 minutes, then cut into squares.

To cook the pasta
Cook pasta in boiling salted water, a few squares at a time, for 4 minutes. Remove and drop immediately into cold water. Drain and spread on a clean cloth to dry. Repeat until all squares are done.

Make a tomato sauce of your choice, the simpler the better.

Mushroom and Ham Filling
450 g/1 lb mushrooms, chopped
225 g/½ lb cooked Limerick ham, diced
½ onion, chopped
butter
2 tbsp/2½ US tbsp olive oil
Parmesan cheese, freshly grated
salt and ground black pepper

Sauté chopped mushrooms, diced ham and onion in butter and olive oil until all ingredients are cooked. Leave to cool. Add freshly-grated Parmesan and season to taste. Place about 2 tbsp/2½ US tbsp of filling on each pasta square and roll it carefully. Arrange filled cannelloni in a shallow buttered baking dish. Cover with tomato sauce, sprinkle with grated Parmesan and bake in a slow oven (150°C/325°F/gas 3) for about 30 minutes. Serve with a crisp salad. Bueno appetito!

MEATBALLS IN TOMATO SAUCE WITH RICE

1 large onion, finely chopped
4 tbsp/5 US tbsp fresh white breadcrumbs
115 ml/4 fl oz/½ cup single cream
225 g/½ lb lean minced (ground) beef
225 g/½ lb minced pork
1 egg, beaten
1 tbsp/1½ US tbsp parsley, chopped
1 glass dry white wine
1 tin tomatoes, chopped, reserving juice
salt and pepper
olive oil and butter for frying
flour
450 g/1 lb/2¼ cups Uncle Ben or basmati rice

Heat olive oil and butter in a frying pan. Add the chopped onion and fry gently over a low heat until soft. Soak the breadcrumbs in the cream and mix gently with a fork until soft. Now combine the onions, soaked breadcrumbs, meat, egg and parsley in a large bowl. Season to taste and mix well. Form the meat into small balls and roll them in flour. Heat more olive oil in a large frying pan. Add the meatballs and fry over medium heat until they are brown all over, shaking frequently. Add the glass of wine and let it evaporate. Then put in the chopped tomatoes and juice and cook for a few minutes. Cover and simmer for 30 minutes. Meanwhile, cook the rice. When ready, shape it into a ring on a serving dish. Place meatballs in the centre and serve.

BAKED PEARS IN WHITE WINE

4 pears
dry white wine to cover
sugar

to serve: *whipped cream*

Peel pears and place in an ovenproof baking dish along with the dry white wine and sugar. Cover and bake in a moderate oven (180°C/350°F/gas 4) for 45 minutes. Serve with whipped cream.

Ballyvolane was built in 1728 and modified in early Italianate style more than a century later. It is a country mansion surrounded by its own farmland in a setting of magnificent trees, wooded grounds and formal gardens. The home of the Green family since the 1950s, it is now run as a country house which is open to visitors.

Ballyvolane House,
Castlelyons,
Co. Cork.

Tel: Fermoy, (025) 36349
Fax: (025) 36781

AVOCADO AND PRAWNS WITH CHEESE SAUCE

225 g/8 oz prawns/small shrimp
2 avocados, halved
30 g/1 oz/2 tbsp flour
30 g/1 oz/¼ stick butter
170 ml/6 fl oz/⅔ cup milk
pinch of cayenne pepper
¼ teaspoon mustard
a little freshly-grated nutmeg
85 g/3 oz/¾ cup cheddar cheese, grated

To make the sauce, melt butter, add flour and stir for 2 minutes on low heat. Gradually add milk, stirring all the time. Simmer for 3 minutes. Stir in cayenne, mustard and nutmeg. Finally add the cheese and stir until melted. Add prawns to the sauce just before dividing the mixture into the 4 avocado halves. Brown under the grill/broiler and serve immediately. Also good with crab meat.

Merna Green

ROAST DUCKLING WITH RED WINE AND ORANGE SAUCE

1 x 2¼ kg/5 lb duckling
2 large oranges
salt and pepper
2 tbsp/2½ US tbsp honey
1 tbsp/1¼ US tbsp boiling water } *mixed together*

Sauce
280 ml/½ pint/1¼ cups red wine
2 tbsp/2½ US tbsp tomato ketchup
2 tsp/2½ US tsp Worcestershire sauce
2 level tbsp/2½ US tbsp brown sugar
1 rounded tsp/1¼ US tsp cornflour (corn starch)
2 tbsp/2½ US tbsp water } *mixed together*

Orange Strips
2 tbsp/2½ US tbsp brandy
2 oranges

Wipe duckling all over to dry. Wipe the inside with paper towel and season inside with salt and pepper. Cut away all excess fat. Prick the skin and rub with salt. Cut the unpeeled orange into chunks and place in the cavity. Place duckling on a wire rack in a large roasting tin and roast at 190°C/375°F/gas 5 for 1 hour, half an hour on each side. Remove duck from oven and cut into 4 pieces. Brush each piece with the honey mixture and return to the oven for half an hour.

To make orange strips, peel the skin thinly from the oranges and cut into fine julienne strips. Place in a saucepan of water and simmer for 20 minutes. Strain off liquid and set strips aside.

To make the sauce, squeeze juice from the oranges and place in a saucepan with the wine, ketchup, Worcestershire sauce and sugar. Bring to the boil and stir in the cornflour/corn starch. Simmer for a few minutes. Just before serving, add the brandy and orange strips to the sauce.

CHICKEN TERRINE

Serves 12 for a starter

1 x 2¼ kg/5 lb chicken, uncooked
450 g/1 lb pork sausage meat
1 large onion, sliced
3 tbsp/3¾ US tbsp chopped parsley or mixed herbs
1 egg, beaten
2 tbsp/2½ US tbsp chicken stock
salt and pepper
4-5 thin streaky rashers/bacon slices

Skin the chicken. Remove flesh and cut into chunks. Mince/grind the chicken, sausage meat, onion and parsley in food processor until thoroughly mixed. Add salt and pepper to taste, beaten egg and the stock. Line the bottom of a 1 kg/2 lb loaf tin with the streaky rashers/bacon slices. Add the chicken mixture and cover with foil. Bake in a moderate oven (180°C/350°F/gas 4) in a pan of water for 2 hours. Cool thoroughly. Serve with plain crackers or thin slices of toast.

CHOCOLATE ROULADE

170 g/6 oz/6 blocks plain dark chocolate pieces
5 eggs, separated
170 g/6 oz/⅔ cup sugar
250 ml/½ pint/1¼ cups cream, whipped
icing/confectionery sugar

Melt chocolate carefully with about 1 tbsp water. Cream sugar and egg yolks until fairly thick. Add the melted chocolate. Whisk egg whites until stiff and fold carefully into the chocolate mixture. Line a Swiss roll tin (a cookie sheet with 2½ cm/1" sides) with parchment/waxed paper and spread roulade into tin. Cook at 190°C/375°F/gas 5 for 25-30 minutes. Test to see if it is cooked with a skewer. Remove from oven and cover with a damp, clean dish cloth. Dust a piece of parchment/waxed paper generously with icing/confectionery sugar and turn the roulade onto it. Cover with the whipped cream and roll up. Place on dish and cover with more icing sugar before serving.

There are spellbinding views from the dining room of Belle Isle overlooking the
waters of Upper Lough Erne in Enniskillen. The house was originally the eighteenth-
century home of a soldier, Sir Ralph Gore. In the late 1880s, it was remodelled in the
English Tudor manor house style, including a minstrel's gallery with wooden
balustrades. The house and its estate were bought in 1992 by the Duke of Abercorn
and are now run by the Honourable Brian and Mary Mulholland who let the north
wing, called the Hamilton Wing, with its magnificent double-vaulted entrance, and
several estate houses for self-catering holidays.

Belle Isle Lisbellaw Enniskillen Northern Ireland BT94 5HF
Telephone 0365 87 231 Facsimile 0365 87 261

POACHED PIKE WITH MUSTARD MAYONNAISE

Serves 6

While no one here or in the UK seems to eat pike, the continentals rave over it. I consulted my old recipe books and found that until the eighteenth century, pike was greatly revered in the British Isles and the centre-piece of many a feast, while the salmon was given to the gillies! I decided to experiment and found that poached pike with a mustard mayonnaise could rival any salmon.

♣

First land your pike. Smaller ones are tastier, and about 1 kg/2½ lb is ideal. Clean the pike and remove scales by scraping up the skin of the fish with a flat knife. Leave head and tail on fish.

Place in a fish kettle if you have one; otherwise a large baking dish will do. Cover the fish with lightly-salted water (1½ level teaspoons salt to 1.1 L/2 pints/5 cups water). Add pared rind of 1 lemon, some parsley, mushroom stalks or celery leaves if available, a slice of onion and carrot, a bay leaf and 12 peppercorns. If you like, 125 ml/¼ pint/½ cup white wine can be added to the bouillon.

Bring liquid to boil over moderate heat, then cover pan and lower heat. (If using a dish, it may be placed, covered, in the oven at 180°C/350°F/gas 4.) Simmer, allowing about 10 minutes per pound. Check with a fork to see if the fish flakes, then you will know it is cooked.

Lift out carefully onto a large serving dish. Serve warm or cold with mustard mayonnaise.

MUSTARD MAYONNAISE

This can be made stronger or milder, depending on taste.

2 egg yolks
¼ tsp English mustard
1 tsp/1¼ US tsp wine vinegar
280 ml/½ pint/1¼ cups vegetable oil

♣

Put these in food processor for a minute or until well-blended and pale in colour. With food processor still spinning, slowly pour in the vegetable oil. (I use mainly sunflower, but add some olive oil or one of the nut oils to add depth.) When the mayonnaise is thick and creamy, switch off processor, add 2 tbsp/2½ US tbsp vinegar, ½ tsp salt, 1-2 tsp/1 US tsp English mustard (adjust to taste), freshly-ground green peppercorns if available (otherwise black). Turn on food processor for just 1 minute to finish. Serve the dish with new potatoes and green salad.

STIR-FRY PIKE WITH GINGER

A good-natured recipe which can be run up in minutes.

1-1½ kg/2-3 lb pike, cleaned

♣

Lightly poach the pike in a fish kettle if you have one, just covering with water and adding lemon rind, celery, a generous spoonful of salt and pepper. When cooked (so skin peels away easily), remove from heat and remove skin and bones from the fish.

The flesh is nicely firm, so you should be left with reasonably chunky pieces. At this stage, either freeze the fish in a bag for use as a wonderful standby when you're in a hurry or proceed.

2 tbsp/2½ US tbsp olive oil
1 large onion, sliced and chopped
2 garlic cloves, sliced finely
30-50 g/1-2 oz/¼-⅓ cup crystallised ginger pieces (depending on taste)
15-30 ml/1-2 oz/2-3 US tbsp soya sauce (avoid heavy soya which has been adulterated with monosodium glutamate)
chopped parsley

♣

Put oil into frying pan and place over moderate heat. Add onion and garlic. When they begin to soften, add soya sauce and pike pieces. Stir regularly. You may need to add more soya if you're using a 'thin' brand. After about 3 minutes, add ginger and continue stirring for 1 minute. Toss chopped parsley on top and serve with noodles or rice, flavoured with lemon juice, black pepper and butter, and a crisp salad.

The stir-fry pike is also very good reheated if any is left over, as it develops a wonderful flavour which is guaranteed to convert even an avowed fish-hater. (For colour, add 1 chopped red pepper to the dish, adding it at the onion stage.)

PHEASANT WITH LAYERED POTATOES

With fishing, shooting and outdoor activities part of daily routine, it seems only natural to enjoy a healthy diet to complement this. One of our staples in the winter season is pheasant, and this simple recipe never fails to produce a succulent meal.

Roast pheasant by placing it upside-down in a roasting pan. Pour 570 ml/ 1 pint/2½ cups liquid – wine and water (about half and half) or stock – over it and place in a very hot oven (225°C/425°F/gas 7) for 20 minutes. Baste, then place in a slow oven (125°C/250°F/gas 2) for 2 hours. Remove from oven, baste and turn the pheasant the right way round. Cover with some bacon slices and finish by placing again in a very hot oven for 20 minutes.

For the gravy, skim any fat off the meat juices and add some vegetable water, plus a tablespoon of wine. Serve with layered potatoes.

Layered Potatoes

As a rough guide, I choose 1 large potato per person and add an extra one or two if they look hungry. Use 1 onion per 4 potatoes. Wash, peel, then slice onions and potatoes very thinly. Parboil in a saucepan of lightly-salted water for about 5 minutes. Drain. Take a large, shallow baking dish, butter the base and pour in enough milk to cover base. Place the drained potato and onion slices in the dish and arrange so the vegetables lie flat. Pour over just enough milk to cover but not drown the potatoes and onion. Sprinkle with Parmesan cheese, black pepper and a little salt. Dot with butter and place in oven at 180°C/350°F/gas 4 for about 30-45 minutes, until done. To add colour to the meal, serve with carrots and broccoli.

CHOCOLATE ORANGE BOMBE

Serves 6

In the summer, with the plentiful supply of our own fresh eggs and the wonderful local milk, we have the main ingredients for a family favourite which always looks impressive.

Ice Cream Base
570 ml/1 pint/2½ cups creamy milk or half milk/half cream
1 vanilla pod
2 egg yolks
55 g/2 oz/2 US tbsp caster sugar

Put the vanilla pod and milk in a small pan and bring almost to the boil. Then leave for the flavours to gel, off the heat, for 15 minutes. Remove vanilla pod.

Cream egg yolks and sugar until pale. Then stir in milk and strain into a fresh saucepan. Place on a gentle heat, stirring all the time, until the mixture thickens enough to coat the back of a wooden spoon. Pour in equal quantities into two bowls.

Into one, add 1 tbsp/1½ US tbsp orange-flavoured liqueur or, if you prefer, 1 tsp/1¼ US tsp orange essence. Set on one side to cool.

Into the other, stir in a chocolate paste made from 1 heaped tbsp/ 1½ US tbsp cocoa, mixed with 1 dessertspoon/1 US tbsp warm water. A teaspoon of Tia Maria or brandy enhances the flavour, but is optional.

If you have used half milk/half cream, whip the cream lightly and fold it into the two cooled custards. Spoon into suitable freezing containers, cover and set in the freezing compartment until half frozen. Remove from freezer and whisk the ice creams thoroughly, then coat the inside of a pudding basin-shaped container with the white ice cream. Return to freezer. When sufficiently hard, fill the centre with the chocolate ice cream and return to freezer. Remove from bowl by plunging it under a hot tap/faucet for a few seconds.

BROWN BREAD ICE CREAM

4 egg yolks
115 g/4 oz/½ cup caster sugar or half caster, half demerara
2-3 drops vanilla essence
425 ml/¾ pint/1½ cups milk
55 g/2 oz/1 cup dry brown breadcrumbs
140 ml/5 fl oz/¾ cup double cream

♣

Whisk egg yolks, caster sugar, vanilla and milk, then heat in a *bain-marie**
to make custard (ready when it coats the back of a spoon). Remove from
heat and cool. Then either put in an ice cream maker for about 20 minutes
or freeze until mushy (1½ hours). Meanwhile, gently toast the breadcrumbs
under the grill/broiler and set aside to cool. If using demerara as well as
caster sugar, add demerara to cooled crumbs. Whisk cream till it forms
peaks. Fold cream and crumbs mixture into lightly frozen ice cream and
either continue for 5 minutes in ice cream maker or freeze it. After 1 hour,
beat it, then cover, seal and freeze. To serve, place for ½ hour in fridge so it
isn't too frozen. Decorate it with violet flowers or serve with strawberries.

One way of using up all those egg whites is to make *Langues de Chat*.
This recipe makes about 20 cats' tongues.

55 g/2 oz/½ stick butter
55 g/2 oz/2 tbsp caster sugar
55 g/2 oz/4 tbsp plain flour
2 egg whites

♣

Beat butter and sugar for 2-3 minutes. Beat in egg whites and then flour.
(You can use a food processor.) Grease and flour a baking tray.
Use 2 spoons for speed (or a forcing bag if you have one) to make finger-
length shapes of the mixture on the tray. Cook at 220°C/425°F/gas 7 for
4-5 minutes until just lightly browned around the edges. Remove from tray
and cool on a wire rack.

* *Bain-marie:* a large deep tray filled with hot water into which dishes requiring slow cooking
in the oven are placed; also used for keeping soups and sauces warm.

Bermingham House was built on the site of a ruined fourteenth-century castle
belonging to John de Bermingham, the first Earl of Louth. In the nineteenth century,
it became the seat of a renowned huntsman, John Dennis, who founded the Galway
Blazers, a famous Irish fox hunt. His great-great-grand niece is the present owner;
Lady Mollie Cusack Smith became the first woman master of hounds exactly a
century later. Master of the hunt for thirty-eight seasons, the celebrated Lady Cusack
Smith continues to breed her own hounds. Hospitality also has a long history at
Bermingham, and the annual hunt ball, held on the second Friday after Christmas, is
one of the year's social highlights in the west of Ireland.

**BERMINGHAM HOUSE
TUAM**

OXTAIL STEW

*3 oxtails
butter, salt and flour
1 large onion, sliced
1 clove garlic, chopped finely
140 ml/¼ pint/⅔ cup red wine (or sherry or Martini)
850 ml/1½ pints/3¾ cups stock
3 tins tomatoes
2½ tbsp/3¼ US tbsp tomato purée
12 cloves*

Roll oxtail segments in flour with a teaspoon of salt and brown in melted butter in a deep pan. Place in a casserole dish. In the same pan, sauté the onion and garlic, add wine and reduce over high heat, stirring all the time. Add stock, tomatoes (juice and all), tomato purée and cloves and pour over oxtails in casserole dish. Bring all to the boil and then cover and cook in a slow, simmering oven (top left in a 4-oven Aga) for 4½ hours. Lift oxtails out with a slotted spoon and place in serving dish. Blot off excess fat with kitchen paper and pour the sauce over them before serving.

CHRISTMAS CAKE

(Using 'K' Beater)

225 g/8 oz/2 sticks butter
225 g/8 oz/1¾ cups brown sugar
1 dessertspoon/1½ US tbsp treacle or molasses
285 g/10 oz/2½ cups wholemeal flour
4 eggs
1 tsp/1¼ US tsp mixed spice
1 tsp/1¼ US tsp powdered cinnamon
½ tsp/¾ US tsp salt
115 g/4 oz/¾ cup glacé cherries
450 g/1 lb/2 cups currants
450 g/1 lb/2 cups sultanas
170 g/6 oz/1 cup raisins
55 g/2 oz/½ cup mixed peel
55 g/2 oz/½ cup almonds, chopped
brandy, rum or sherry

♣

Prepare a 20 cm/8" cake tin by lining with a double thickness of greased/waxed paper.

Place the butter and the sugar in the warmed bowl and cream on speed 2, gradually increasing to speed 4-6 until white and fluffy (3-4 minutes).

Add the treacle/molasses. Then add the eggs, one at a time. Increase the speed to 8 after the addition of the first egg and add the others at about 10 second intervals. Turn to maximum speed after the last addition and beat for 30 seconds. Reduce speed to 3 and add sifted flour, spices and salt, then fruit and nuts. Switch off as soon as all ingredients are incorporated and turn into the prepared tin. Bake in a slow oven (150°C/300°F/gas 2) for 3½-4 hours.

Remove from oven and leave the cake in the tin for 15 minutes. Then turn it onto a wire rack to cool. When the cake is cold, turn it upside-down. Pierce in several places with a fine steel knitting needle and pour a wine glass of brandy, rum or sherry over and allow it to soak in. To store, wrap the cake in thick, greaseproof/waxed paper and place in an airtight container.

CLOSHEENS MARINIÈRE

(QUEEN SCALLOPS)

'Closheens' comes from the Irish word, *cluaisini*, the smaller 'queen'
scallop which is about 5 cm/2" in diameter.

40 closheens
280 ml/½ pint/ 1 cup dry white wine
½ onion, finely chopped
1 dessertspoon/2 US tbsp parsley, finely chopped
sprig of fresh thyme
salt and pepper to taste
beurre manié (optional)

♣

Place the closheens in a saucepan with the white wine, onion, parsley and
thyme. Cook very quickly until the closheens are just open. Remove from
the pan using a slotted spoon. Remove the beards and black parts and dip
quickly in water to clean. Strain the wine sauce and put back the cleaned
closheens. Add salt and pepper to taste. If liked, *beurre manié* may be used
to thicken the sauce. This is made by rubbing together equal quantities of
butter and flour, and is sprinkled gradually into the hot liquid.

Once known as Parsonstown, Birr Castle is one of the finest demesnes in Ireland and has been in the ownership of the Parsons family for fourteen generations. The castle's unique culinary records date back to the 1600s, and the handwritten cookery and other notebooks have been carefully preserved, giving insights into food and eating habits in Ireland over many centuries. The house was considerably extended in the early 1800s and reoriented so that its front faced the parkland rather than the town. A giant telescope, once the largest in the world, was erected here in the 1840s by the third earl who was an astronomer. Today, the magnificent and varied gardens of Birr Castle are open to the public.

Birr Castle

PIGEON SOUP

This recipe comes from Alice, 2nd Countess of Rosse, and dates back to about 1800.

Take only the breast and wings of the pigeon. Put them in a stewpan with a sliced carrot and onion and a bunch of herbs, 2 or 3 peppercorns and cloves. Cover with stock. Boil until tender, then pass through a fine sieve. Put back in the pan, and make it very hot before serving. Add a little seasoning and a tablespoonful of cream.

Alison Rosse

Birr Castle, Birr, Co. Offaly

VENISON IN GUINNESS

Good for a shooting lunch.

oil for cooking
1.3 kg/3 lb stewing venison (preferably from the shoulder or the neck, or
anywhere that you will not need the meat for roasting etc.)
1½ onions, sliced
2 tbsp/2½ US tbsp brown sugar
bouquet garni
3 cloves garlic, chopped small
salt and pepper
280 ml/½ pint/1¼ cups beef stock (I use a stock cube)
570 ml/1 pint/2½ cups Guinness

♣

Marinate the venison in wine for a day or two before preparing. I find that freezing venison tenderises it – in the past, it would be hung for several days which had the same effect. Brown the chopped venison in hot oil. Remove the meat and stir in the onions. Add salt (not too much), pepper and garlic. Heat stock and pour over venison and onions. Add Guinness to cover and simmer slowly for 2-3 hours. Boil rapidly at the end to reduce the liquid by two-thirds. Serve with mashed potatoes and red cabbage.

CODLING CREAM

This is a recipe from Dorothy Parsons, just as she herself wrote it in the 1660s. We have modernised the ingredients and method. The 'codlings' referred to are cooking apples.

Take a quantity of codlings and boyle them in white wine till they are soft, then draine all the liquor from them and straine all the pap through a strainer, then take a pint of creame, boyle it and thick it with two yolks of eggs, and whilst it is hott putt in the pap and keepe it contunually stiring untill it bee cold. You must season the pap with rose water and sugar before you mingle it.

8 cooking apples, peeled and cut up
280 ml/½ pint/1¼ cups white wine
280 ml/½ pint/1¼ cups water
570 ml/1 pint/2½ cups cream
2 egg yolks
1 tbsp/1¼ US tbsp rose water (optional)
85 g/3 oz/3 tbsp sugar

Peel and cut up the apples, then cook them in the wine and water until soft. Strain off the liquid, then mash up or liquidise the apples and add the sugar. Whip the cream, then whip the egg yolks and fold into the cream. Fold the egg and cream into the apple. Finally, if you would like the genuine seventeenth-century flavour, stir in the rose water. Serve in glasses with shortbread or biscuits.

Busherstown House was built on the site of an O'Carroll castle. The façade is typical
of the Gothic revival period and the reception rooms have beautiful cornice
mouldings. The Rudd family runs a home-produced bacon business and recently
converted part of their yard into a workshop area where various crafts are taught.

CHICORY AND BACON

This is a delicious starter or supper dish.

8 medium chicory
8 thinly-sliced rashers/bacon slices

Cheese Sauce
1 level tbsp/1¼ US tbsp flour
115 ml/4 fl oz/⅔ cup milk
30 g/1 oz/¼ stick butter
1 tsp/1¼ US tsp Lakeshore mustard
85 g/3 oz/¾ cup mature Cashel blue cheese
85 g/3 oz/¾ cup mature Irish cheddar

Wrap each chicory in a rasher/bacon slice and place in shallow pyrex or ovenproof dish. Make cheese sauce by whisking flour into cold milk in saucepan and slowly bringing to boil. Add butter and mustard and cook for 3 minutes. Crumble in Cashel blue cheese and half of cheddar. Pour sauce over the chicory and bake in a moderate oven (180°C/350°F/gas 4) for 45 minutes. Ten minutes before it is cooked, add the remaining cheese.

CHEESY PORK CHOPS

4 well-trimmed pork chops
salt and pepper
1 tbsp/1¼ US tbsp olive oil
1 tbsp/1¼ US tbsp melted butter
115 g/4 oz/1 cup grated hard cheese (e.g. cheddar)
1 tsp/1¼ US tsp Lakeshore mustard
2 tbsp/2½ US tbsp cream

Season the chops and sauté in olive oil and butter until cooked. Mix together cheese, mustard and cream and spread over the chops which have been placed in a shallow oven dish. Place under the grill/broiler for a few minutes to give a nice finish.

Tip: If you don't have a grill, I find a small butane blow torch does the job beautifully. This can also be used to glaze ham or bacon and does not dry out the joint as the high temperature of an oven does.

MARJORIE'S FLORENTINE FINGERS

115 g/4 oz/4 blocks best cooking chocolate
55 g/2 oz/4 tbsp margarine
115 g/4 oz/4 tbsp caster sugar
1 egg, beaten
115 g/4 oz/1⅔ cups dried coconut
55 g/2 oz/½ cup cherries
55 g/2 oz/½ cup raisins
45 g/1½ oz/⅓ cup shelled walnuts, chopped

Line a 18 cm/7" baking tray with tin foil. Melt chocolate slowly, then spread evenly over the foil. Cream margarine and sugar. Beat in the egg, a little at a time. Stir in coconut, chopped cherries, raisins and walnuts. Spread the mixture over the chocolate. Bake in a moderate oven (180°C/350°F/gas 4) for 30 minutes, or until the top looks golden. When cool, peel the tin foil from the chocolate and cut into fingers. Keep in air-tight container and refrigerate.

Upside-down Pudding

1 x 400 g/14 oz tin sliced peaches
2 tbsp/2½ US tbsp golden syrup/Karo syrup
85 g/3 oz/¾ stick butter or margarine
85 g/3 oz/3 tbsp caster sugar
2 small eggs
55 g/2 oz/4 tbsp self-raising flour (or soft white flour sieved/sifted
with ¼ US tsp baking powder)
2 large carrots, finely grated
175 ml/6 oz/⅔ cup natural yogurt

♣

Put golden/Karo syrup in a warmed 15 cm/6" deep cake tin. Strain the peaches, keeping the juice. Arrange the peaches on top of the syrup which has now spread over the base of the tin.

Make cake mixture in the usual way. Cream sugar and butter, add eggs and mix well. Add flour and mix. Then add the grated carrot. Spoon mixture over peaches. Bake for 35-40 minutes at 180°C/350°F/gas 4. When cooked, put a knife around the edge of the tin. Then turn the tin upside-down onto a plate.

Mix together the yogurt and peach juice and serve with the pudding as a sauce.

A castellated country house set in magnificent parkland in the Irish lakelands,
Carrigglas Manor originally belonged to the bishops of Ardagh in the seventeenth
century. It is now the ancestral home of the Lefroy family who rebuilt it in the Tudor
Gothic style in the mid-nineteenth century. Designed by the renowned architect
Daniel Robertson, this imposing mansion retains much of its original plasterwork,
furniture and artefacts. Jeffry and Tessa Lefroy like to receive visitors as personal
guests and their cuisine is based on traditional Irish food cooked with great flair.

FILLETS OF MACKEREL
WITH SWEET AND SOUR BEETROOT SAUCE

2 medium beetroots (beets), cooked
4 large or 8 small fillets of fresh mackerel
flour
salt and freshly-ground black pepper
70 g/2½ oz/¾ stick butter
1 tbsp/1¼ US tbsp vegetable oil
3 tbsp/3¾ US tbsp white wine vinegar or cider vinegar
2 tbsp/2½ US tbsp brown granulated sugar

to garnish: *1 tbsp/1¼ US tbsp parsley, finely chopped*

♣

Peel the beetroots, cut into small dice and set aside. Lightly coat mackerel fillets with seasoned flour. Melt half the butter with the oil. Add mackerel fillets and cook over medium heat, turning once, until fillets are golden brown and cooked through. Transfer to heated serving dish or individual plates. Pour over juices from the pan and keep warm while making the sauce.

To make the sauce, melt the remaining butter in saucepan. Add 1 tsp/1¼ US tsp salt, the vinegar and the sugar and stir over low heat until the sugar has melted. Add beetroot dice and toss over medium-high heat until sauce is very hot. Spoon sauce over the mackerel fillets and dust with finely-chopped parsley before serving with home-made brown yeast bread and butter.

BRAISED LOIN OF PORK WITH VEGETABLES

1 kg/2½ lb loin of pork, boned and seasoned (keep the bone)
1 clove garlic, halved
½ tsp/¾ US tsp diced oregano
2 tbsp/2½ US tbsp sesame seeds
4 tbsp/5 US tbsp olive oil
1 large onion
175 g/6 oz cabbage, shredded
225 g/8 oz parsnips, diced
350 g/12 oz potatoes, peeled and diced
salt and freshly-ground black pepper
little fresh sage and thyme, finely chopped
cider (hard cider in US)
2 tbsp/2½ US tbsp fresh orange juice
150 ml/¼ pint/⅔ cup single or double cream
1½ tbsp/2 US tbsp parsley, finely chopped

♣

Score pork fat with sharp knife. Rub in the garlic, seasoning and oregano. Sprinkle with sesame seeds, pour over half the olive oil, place in a heavy casserole dish and roast in hot oven (220°C/425°F/gas 7) for 20 minutes to seal in juices.

Peel and chop onion. Shred cabbage. Peel and cut parsnips and potatoes into 2½ cm/1" cubes.

Remove pork from oven and surround it with the vegetables. Place bone on top of vegetables, season further and sprinkle with thyme and sage. Pour in enough cider to come half-way up the vegetables. Add orange juice and sprinkle with the remaining oil.

Cover with 2 layers of foil and the casserole lid. Cook in moderate oven (180°C/350°F/gas 4) for 1¼ hours, removing foil for last 15 minutes.

Remove pork from oven and cut into thin slices. Add cream and parsley to vegetables and mix lightly. Arrange vegetables on shallow serving dish and place slices of pork on top.

LEMON NEW POTATOES

A nice sharp, lemony way of serving new potatoes.

675-900 g/1½-2 lb small new potatoes
1 lemon
45 g/1½ oz/½ stick butter
2-3 tsp/3-4 US tsp fresh dill or fennel
salt and freshly-ground black pepper

♣

Wash or scrape potatoes. Place in saucepan and cover with lightly-salted boiling water. Add a strip of lemon rind. Boil until half cooked, then pour off most of the water, leaving just enough to cover base of pan (about 2½ cm/1"). Add most of the juice of a lemon and finish cooking. Drain and toss in hot butter. Season and finish with chopped fennel or dill and a final squeeze of lemon.

ELDERFLOWER SORBET

We make this sorbet in early summer when the trees are laden with elderflowers. It has a delightful, elusive taste.

600 ml/1 pint/2½ cups water
225 g/8 oz/1 cup granulated sugar
3 lemons, rind and juice
3-4 elderflower heads

♣

Combine sugar and water in a very clean pan and heat slowly, stirring until the sugar dissolves. Boil hard, without stirring, for 5-6 minutes. Remove from heat, throw in elderflower heads and pared lemon rinds and infuse for 2-3 hours. Strain liquid and add lemon juice to taste.

Freeze in the usual way, beating the edges into the middle as they thicken. When it is set quite firm, process or beat hard until soft, smooth and light. Turn into a container and refreeze. Mellow in fridge for ½ hour before serving.

Cleggan Lodge is a 'cottage orné' style house, with a thatched roof and eyebrow windows. Built around 1820 by Earl O'Neill of Shane's Castle, it was one of a number of similar residences which the earl built in County Antrim. These were located at different beauty spots where he and his bachelor brother entertained ladies and gambled. Cleggan was also used as a shooting lodge during the summer season because of its proximity to the grouse moors of north Antrim. The house had fallen into ruin when the present owner's grandfather, Sir Hugh O'Neill, 1st Lord Rathcavan, bought it from his father in 1927. It was restored and remodelled to include kitchen and nursery wings. Cleggan Lodge looks onto the famous mountain of Slemish where St Patrick is said to have herded swine as a boy.

TARTE AUX TOMATES

Good as a starter or main course.

puff pastry (frozen)
450 g/1 lb tomatoes (not too ripe)
tarragon mustard
grated cheddar cheese (about 30-40 g/1-1½ oz/½ cup)
olive oil
salt and black pepper, freshly ground

♣

Roll out the pastry and line a 25-30 cm/10-12" tin with it. Press firmly on the base and sides, then prick all over with a fork.

Spread the tarragon mustard evenly (with the back of a spoon) then sprinkle the cheddar cheese over the mustard. Finally, place the thinly-sliced tomatoes on top. Sprinkle a few drops of olive oil on top of the tomatoes and season with salt and pepper. Cook in oven (200°C/400°F/gas 6) for approximately ½ hour or until pastry is golden.

Gita O'Neill

LOUGH NEAGH EELS

♣

An old recipe, this dish was the main course or 'tea' for Lough Neagh eel fishermen returning to their shore base, cooked on a fire of driftwood and sometimes with pieces of bacon.

It would be wrong to call this eel dish fried or grilled, as it is a combination of both. Eels contain a lot of fat/oil, so get some fresh (live) eels. An eel is easy to prepare. Put a nail through the head on a wooden wall. Cut the skin around the neck and pull the skin off like a sock. Put salt on your hands if it is slippery. Cut off the head, remove the guts, cut the body into 2 cm/¾" pieces. Put them in a large heavy (cast iron is the best) pan and cook over a slow heat for 2 hours, shaking and turning occasionally. It is best over a peat fire in a brazier which gives the right level of smouldering heat. No doubt it also gives a sniff of peat flavour too. Good for a summer barbeque.

CLAFOUTIS

2 eggs
100 g/3½ oz/3½ tbsp granulated sugar
100 g/3½ oz/⅔ cup plain flour
250 ml/9 fl oz/1¼ cups milk
450 g/1 lb fruit in season: cherries, apricots, plums, apples (stoned and peeled where necessary)

Break the eggs into a bowl and add the sugar. Whisk until creamy, then add flour and milk (warm but not boiled). Add fruit to the mixture. Pour into an ovenproof dish and cook in oven (200°C/400°F/gas 6) until brown. To find out if it is cooked, prick a knife in the middle. If it comes out clean, the pudding is ready.

Clohamon is a delightful two-storey Georgian house set in 180 acres and
surrounded by beechwoods and gardens containing many rare trees and plants. Set
on a hill, the house has a panoramic view of Mount Leinster and the land is also
home to an internationally renowned Connemara pony stud. Food at Clohamon is
based on home-grown and local produce.

Clohamon House,
Bunclody,
Co. Wexford.
Tel: 054-77253
Fax: 054-77956

DEEP-FRIED COURGETTE FRITTERS WITH YOGURT AND BLUE CHEESE

Serves 6 as a starter, 4 as a main course. Suitable for vegetarians.
Use a mixture of vegetables if you like, including cauliflower, broccoli,
aubergine/eggplant, red and green peppers.

6 small courgettes/zucchini, cut into tiny fingers

Batter
115 g/4 oz/1 cup wholemeal flour
sea salt and freshly-ground black pepper
1 free range egg
1 tbsp/1¼ US tbsp sunflower oil
2 tsp/2½ US tsp cider vinegar
sunflower oil for frying

Yogurt and Blue Cheese Sauce
6 tbsp/½ cup natural yogurt
85 g/3 oz/¾ cup Cashel blue cheese
2 tbsp/2½ US tbsp mayonnaise
black pepper, freshly ground

Make up batter. Dip courgette/zucchini fingers into the batter and fry in
deep-fat fryer at 190°C/375°F/gas 6 in batches until crisp and golden. Serve
hot with yogurt and blue cheese sauce. Sprinkle with chopped flat-leaved
parsley and garlic chives.

ROAST LOIN OF FREE-RANGE PORK WITH APPLES, CARAMELISED WITH IRISH MIST

loin of pork, around 1 kg/2½ lb
olive oil to brush
sea salt
2 Cox or Golden Delicious apples
30 g/1 oz/¼ stick butter
1 dsp/1½ US tbsp demerara sugar
juice of 1 lemon
2 dsp/3 US tbsp Irish Mist

to garnish: *apple mint or lemon balm*

♣

Score the pork rind and rub with sea salt. Place in a roasting tin which has been brushed with a little olive oil. Roast in a hot oven (220°C/475°F/gas 7) for about 35 minutes per lb.

Peel, core and slice the apples and cook gently in a pan with the butter. Add the demerara sugar, stir gently and cook for a couple of minutes until it begins to caramelise. Then add the lemon juice and Irish Mist and cook until syrupy. To serve, remove the crisp, scored crackling from the pork and divide into fingers. Carve the pork thinly and arrange three slices in a fan shape on a warm plate. Add the warm caramelised apples and garnish with apple mint or lemon balm. Serve with vegetables in season.

RHUBARB AND HONEY JELLIES WITH AMARETTO SABAYON

Serves 6

900 g/2 lb fresh rhubarb
4 tbsp/5 US tbsp water
3 tbsp/3¾ US tbsp Wexford honey
1 sachet of gelatine

Cut rhubarb into 2½ cm/1" lengths and put into a heavy saucepan with water. Cook until soft and juicy, about 30 minutes. Strain off juice into measuring jug. You will need 570 ml/1 pint/2½ cups of liquid, so if short, put required amount of water with pulp and boil again for 5 minutes. Add honey to hot liquid.

Meanwhile, put 3 tbsp/3¾ US tbsp of water in a small bowl, sprinkle on the gelatine and let it sponge for a minute. Then put into microwave on low for 1 minute to dissolve. *Do not boil.* Stir dissolved gelatine into cooled rhubarb liquid. Lightly brush 6 small moulds or ramekins with sunflower oil. Pour in jelly and leave to set in fridge for at least 4 hours.

AMARETTO SABAYON

2 free range egg yolks
1 tbsp/1¼ US tbsp caster sugar
2 generous tbsp/2½ US tbsp honey
1-1½ tbsp/1¼-2 US tbsp Amaretto liqueur
3-4 tbsp/4-5 US tbsp natural yogurt
115 g/4 oz/1 cup toasted almonds

Whisk yolks, sugar and honey until thick and creamy. Add liqueur and yogurt. Stand bowl over hot water and whisk until increased in volume. Pour around jellies, sprinkle with toasted almonds and garnish with a sprig of fresh garden mint.

Note: Jellies can be made with summer fruits and also look very nice made with blood oranges.

Built on the site of an old castle of the Pale, Clonmannon was originally the home of Sir Abraham Yarner, a Cromwellian planter. Cromwell himself is said to have lived here during one of his sojourns in Ireland. Clonmannon changed ownership around 1800 and the present building, a Queen Anne house, was left derelict for 150 years until the whole estate was bought in 1968 by the present owner who restored it completely in the late 1980s. During the recent restoration, an old moat and the remains of a garrison yard were discovered around the house.

MUSSEL SOUP EXTRAVAGANZA

I find the sparkling wine gives this soup a real gourmet quality.

1¾ kg/4 lbs fresh mussels (or two net bags), cleaned and bearded
1 tbsp/1¼ US tbsp Italian virgin olive oil
1 onion, chopped
1 clove garlic, finely chopped
handful of parsley, chopped
½ bottle sparkling white wine
100 ml/4 fl oz/½ cup cream
pinch of cumin
black pepper, freshly ground

to garnish: *parsley or coriander*

♣

Pre-heat a large saucepan and add Italian virgin olive oil. Fry the onion and garlic gently, then add parsley and half glass of wine. Then add mussels, cover and boil for approximately 5 minutes or until shells have opened. Strain the mussels and remove them from their shells, keeping aside 4 whole ones for decoration. Chop the remaining mussels and add to the juice. Replace on heat, and season with pepper. Add the cream and a pinch of cumin and bring quickly to the boil. Add the sparkling wine to make up the quantity required and boil for a further 2 minutes. Serve hot, garnished with mussels in their shells and chopped parsley or a sprig of coriander, if available.

Francesco Colonne di Stigliano

Roast Lamb Clonmannon

small-to-medium leg of lamb, shank uncracked
garlic
mint
green olive oil
salt and pepper
lemon
2 onions
1 carrot
1 parsnip, cut in chunks
2 tbsp/2½ US tbsp Cointreau (optional)

Spike joint with slivers of garlic and if feeling completely extravagant, inject the leanest parts with Cointreau. Rub all over with green olive oil and season well with salt, pepper and mint. Place in a heavy roasting dish with the onions, carrot and parsnip. Put on the top shelf of pre-heated oven at 220°C/425°F/gas 7. After 30 minutes, turn the roast over, squeeze half a lemon over it and cook for a further hour approximately.

To make gravy, remove the roast from the pan and keep warm. Discard vegetables if burnt and pour off the fat, retaining approximately 1 tbsp/1¼ US tbsp of juice. Place pan over high heat and add approximately 1 tbsp/1¼ US tbsp flour and brown, stirring well. Add a dash of Irish whiskey (poteen if nobody is looking), the vegetable water and a dash of Worcestershire sauce. Season to taste and finally add half a glass of dry white wine. Serve piping hot with green vegetables and masses of roast potatoes.

VITTORIA AND LUCREZIA'S EXOTIC FRUIT SALAD

This dish is named after Vittoria and Lucrezia, who are a great help.

1 large ripe mango
2 kiwi fruit
4 plums
2 peaches
1 handful of grapes
1 handful of redcurrants (or other seasonal berries)
1 or 2 passion fruit
(Other soft fruit in season may be used. The object is a combination of
sweet and slightly tart flavours.)
1 tbsp/1¼ US tbsp Cointreau or Grand Marnier
30-60 ml/1-2 fl oz/¼ cup sparkling or light white wine
1 tsp/1¼ US tsp sugar

♣

Set aside 2 plums and the passion fruit. Peel (where necessary) and slice (generously) all the rest of the fruit and place in a bowl. Cut the passion fruit into halves and squeeze the contents over the bowl of fruit, spraying the entire contents with the passion fruit seeds and pulp. Stew the 2 plums in a saucepan with the Cointreau, the wine and the sugar. The object is to produce a plummy syrup, so the quantity of wine will depend on the juiciness of the plums. Allow to cool, then strain the juice over the entire bowl and stand for a minimum of 1 hour. Serve with whipped cream presented in a separate bowl.

Home to seven generations of the O'Hara family, the construction of Coopershill began in 1755 and took nearly twenty years to complete. It is said that the fine local stone which was used, known as ashlar, took eight years to quarry and that the bridge across the River Arrow took as much money to build as the basement and ground floor because it kept sinking into the bog and eventually bales of wool had to be used to anchor it. Standing in the centre of a 500-acre wooded estate and farm, Coopershill is close to Lough Arrow and twelve miles from Sligo. It has been open to guests since 1968.

Coopershill,
Riverstown, Co. Sligo
Tel: (071) 65108 Fax: (071) 65466

COURGETTE SOUP WITH GARLIC AND BLUE CHEESE

A blender or food processor is necessary for this recipe. The soup can be made up to two days in advance and will improve in flavour with keeping. Store it in a covered container in the refrigerator. Excellent served chilled in the summertime.

Serves 6

450 g/1 lb courgettes/zucchini, trimmed and sliced
40 g/1½ oz/⅓ stick butter or margarine
1 medium onion, peeled and roughly chopped
2 cloves garlic, skinned and crushed
1.1 L/2 pints/5 cups vegetable stock
2 heaped tsp/2½ US tsp chopped fresh basil
or 1 level tsp/1¼ US tsp dried basil
salt and freshly-ground black pepper
175 g/6 oz/1½ cups blue cheese
150 ml/¼ pint/⅔ cup cream

to garnish: *chopped fresh basil or whole sprigs of basil*

♣

Melt the butter or margarine in a large, heavy-based saucepan. Add the onion and garlic and fry gently for about 5 minutes until soft and lightly coloured. Add the courgettes and cook gently for 10 minutes, shaking the pan and stirring frequently. Pour in the stock and bring slowly to the boil. Then lower the heat and add the basil, with salt and pepper to taste. Cover and simmer gently for 20 minutes, stirring occasionally.

Lindy O'Hara

Meanwhile, remove any rind from the cheese and then dice it. Place in a liquidiser or food processor with all but 4 tablespoons (5 US tbsp) of the cream. Blend to a smooth purée.

Add the hot soup to the machine, a ladleful at a time, and blend to incorporate it with the cheese and cream. Blend again until the purée is really smooth. Return the soup to the rinsed-out pan and reheat gently. Taste and adjust the seasoning. Pour into a soup tureen or individual bowls and swirl the reserved cream on the top. Garnish with basil.

Vegetarian Goulash

2 tbsp/2½ US tbsp olive oil
2 medium onions, sliced
1 dsp/1½ US tbsp wholemeal flour
1 heaped tbsp/1½ US tbsp of paprika
1 x 400 g/14 oz tin tomatoes
280 ml/½ pint/1¼ cups hot water enriched with
1 tsp/1¼ US tsp tomato purée
250 g/8 oz cauliflower sprigs
250 g/8 oz carrots, cut into chunks
250 g/8 oz courgettes/zucchini, cut into chunks
½ green pepper, deseeded and chopped
280 ml/½ pint/1¼ cups sour cream or yogurt
a pinch of cayenne pepper
salt and pepper

Heat the oil in a flameproof dish. Fry the onion until softened, then stir in the flour, most of the paprika and the cayenne pepper. Cook for a minute, then stir in the tomatoes and the water. Bring the sauce to the boil, stirring all the time. Then add all the vegetables. Season with salt and pepper. Cover and put in a pre-heated oven (180°C/350°F/gas 4) for 30-40 minutes. Finally stir in the sour cream or yogurt. Scatter the rest of the paprika on top and serve.

IRISH TEA CAKE

280 ml/½ pint/1¼ cups strong, cold tea
450 g/1 lb/2-2½ cups dried mixed fruits
225 g/8 oz/1 cup demerara sugar
115 g/4 oz/⅔ cup chopped walnuts
115 g/4 oz/⅔ cup glacé cherries, rinsed, dried and quartered
1 large egg, beaten together with 2 tbsp/2½ US tbsp milk
450 g/1 lb/4 cups self-raising flour (or soft white flour sieved/sifted with
1 tsp baking powder)
1 dsp/1½ US tbsp mixed spices

Prepare the fruit by soaking it with the sugar in the cold tea overnight. Next day, stir in the remaining ingredients and put mixture into two well-greased 450 g/1 lb loaf tins. Bake in the centre of a pre-heated oven (170°C/325°F/gas 4) for about 1 hour and 10 minutes, or until golden brown on top and springy to touch in the centre. Then turn it onto a wire rack, right side up. As soon as it is cool, slice across into 1¼ cm/½" slices and serve spread thickly with butter. Also freezes well.

FUDGE

1 kg/2¼ lb/5 cups sugar
250 ml/9 fl oz/1¼ cups milk
125 g/4½ oz/½ cup margarine
1 tin sweetened condensed milk (397 g/14 oz)
1 tsp/1¼ US tsp vanilla essence

♣

Put all the ingredients except the vanilla into a pan and stir well before putting on the stove. Bring slowly to the boil (so that the sugar dissolves slowly without burning) and then boil for 20 to 30 minutes. Test for soft ball (120°C/250°F) with a sugar thermometer or drop a bit of the mixture into some cold water and if it becomes solid, it's set. Remove from heat and add the vanilla essence. Beat well with a wooden spoon until the mixture becomes thick and creamy. Pour into a Swiss roll tin (a cookie sheet with 2½ cm/1" sides) or similar and leave for 10 to 15 minutes to cool. Then cut into squares and leave until really cool before removing and placing in an airtight container.

Cuffsborough was built in 1770 as a land speculation by the young Henry Grattan. It was later sold to the Palmer family, cousins of the founder of the Royal Dublin Society, Thomas Prior of Rathdowney. It is now owned by John Colclough, founder of *The Hidden Ireland* country house association, and his brother. The two are gradually restoring what was an abandoned ruin. John's wife, Alix Gardner, is a well-known cook with her own cookery school in Dublin. She makes good use of the local crab apples, sloes and blackberries as well as Joan Hyland's excellent local Abbey Blue Brie, a cambozola-like soft cheese.

Cuffsborough House

Clough

Laois

AVOCADO AND ABBEY BLUE SALAD

a selection of lettuce leaves – 1 oakleaf, 1 raddichio, 1 lamb's lettuce
2 avocados
1 dsp/1½ US tbsp basil, chopped
55 g/2 oz/½ cup pine nuts
5 sun-dried tomatoes, chopped
225 g/8 oz/2 cups Abbey Blue cheese

Dressing
1 tsp/1¼ US tsp pesto
1 tsp/1¼ US tsp basil, freshly chopped
oil – sunflower or walnut oil } *3 parts oil to 1 part vinegar*
balsamic vinegar

♣

Wash the lettuce and tear the leaves in half. Remove rind from cheese and cut into dice size. Cut the sun-dried tomatoes into 4. Toast the pine nuts. Mix together the salad dressing. Just before serving, slice the avocado and mix the salad ingredients together, placing the avocado and Abbey Blue cheese on top. Sprinkle with extra chopped basil.

SALMON IN FILO PASTRY WITH DILL SAUCE

This is one of my favourite recipes. It is quick and easy and can be served
with Hollandaise sauce or, for the health-minded, try the dill sauce
suggested here.

450 g/1 lb fresh salmon
8 sheets filo pastry
115 g/4 oz/1 stick butter, melted
30 g/1 oz/2 tbsp fresh ginger
2 carrots
1 leek
1 lemon

Dill Sauce
1 tub crème fraîche
1 packet dill or fennel
28 ml/1 fl oz/2 tbsp white wine vinegar

to decorate: *fennel*

Peel the ginger and cut into small, thin strips (remember – it is very hot).
Cut the leek and carrots into julienne strips, place in a saucepan and cook
slowly in a little butter. Cut the salmon into cubes and mix with lemon juice.
Brush one sheet of filo pastry with melted butter, place another sheet on
top and continue for 4 layers. Cut out 2 large squares and place a quarter of
the salmon on each square. Place a little of the julienne of carrots, leeks and
ginger on top. Take the four corners and twist together to form a pouch.
Repeat with 2 more squares of filo pastry and the remaining salmon. Brush
with melted butter. Place in a pre-heated moderate oven (170°C/325°F/
gas 3) for 20 minutes. Turn up for 7 minutes more at a high temperature.

Note: When working with filo pastry, always cover with a damp cloth so it
doesn't dry out.

To make the dill sauce
Chop dill, add crème fraîche and vinegar. Mix well.

To serve, place filo pastry on a warm plate. Serve the sauce on the side with
a sprig of dill.

POTATO CAKES

My mother used to make potato cakes for breakfast using leftover mashed potatoes. She hardly had them out of the pan and they were gone! They can be served for breakfast, lunch or supper.

Makes 12

900 g/2 lb potatoes
170 g/6 oz/1½ cups flour
salt and pepper

Peel the potatoes, bring slowly to the boil and simmer until cooked. Drain, then put back in the pan over the heat to dry out. Mash well and cool. Mix in enough flour so you can roll out the potato mixture. Cut into 12 squares. Heat some oil in a frying pan and fry until a dark golden brown. Sprinkle with salt and pepper and serve immediately.

With its breathtaking mountain and lake setting, Delphi is one of the finest sporting lodges in Ireland. Built in the 1830s on the shores of Doolough, it was originally the hunting estate of the Marquis of Sligo. Since 1988, it has been the home of Peter Mantle, a writer and fisherman, and his wife Jane who is a cordon bleu cook. The magnificently restored house is surrounded by ancient woodlands, rich in flora and fauna, and now has a regular stream of visitors who come for the fishing and the tranquillity, not to mention the good food.

THE DELPHI ESTATE & FISHERY

KILLARY BAY MUSSELS

1¾ kg/4 lb mussels
1 large onion, finely chopped
3 cloves garlic, finely chopped
handful of fresh parsley, chopped
½ pint/1¼ cups dry white wine
½ pint/1¼ cups cream
black pepper
2 tbsp/2½ US tbsp lemon juice

to garnish: *chopped parsley*

Wash mussels in sink under running water and pull off beards and scrape off barnacles. Place onion, garlic, parsley and wine in a large saucepan and bring quickly to the boil. Then simmer for about 5 minutes.

Add mussels to the wine stock, cover and cook on high heat for a further 5 minutes, until the mussels are fully open. Stir with a wooden spoon. Remove mussels with a slotted spoon. Place on a large serving dish and keep warm. Bring liquid back to the boil. Add cream, pepper and lemon juice and boil for 2 minutes more until slightly thickened. Place mussels in warm soup bowls and pour sauce over. Garnish with chopped parsley.

Jane Mantle

LEENANE, Co.GALWAY, IRELAND. TELEPHONE: (095) 42213 or 42245. FAX: (095) 42212

DELPHI SALMON CREAMS WITH LEMON DRESSING

225 g/8 oz smoked salmon
black pepper, freshly ground
140 ml/5 fl oz/⅔ cup milk
140 ml/5 fl oz/⅔ cup cream
yolks of 3 large eggs
1 tbsp/1¼ US tbsp chives/spring onions, chopped
pinch of grated nutmeg

Lemon Dressing
1 tbsp/1¼ US tbsp fresh lemon juice
1 tbsp/1¼ US tbsp olive oil
1 tbsp/1¼ US tbsp wholegrain mustard
salt and black pepper to taste
red oak or iceberg lettuce

Finely chop the salmon and place in small buttered ramekin dishes. Pour cream and milk into mixing bowl, adding egg yolks, chives or spring onions, nutmeg and pepper. Mix thoroughly with a fork. Pour this mixture over the fish in ramekins. Place ramekins in a *bain-marie** and bake at 180°C/350°F/gas 4 on middle shelf of oven for 20-30 minutes or until set and golden brown. Leave ramekins to rest for 20 minutes. To serve, run blade of knife around the edges. Tip each one out into the palm of your hand and turn right way up again on plate. Serve warm (they can be made in advance and gently reheated).

For lemon dressing, measure all ingredients into a jar and shake to mix well. Just before serving, pour enough dressing on the salad to coat the leaves lightly. Arrange the salad around each Delphi salmon cream.

*Bain-marie: a large deep tray filled with hot water into which dishes requiring slow cooking in the oven are placed; also used for keeping soups and sauces warm.

FOCACCIA BREAD WITH SUN-DRIED TOMATOES

340 g/12 oz/3 cups strong white flour
pinch of salt
2 tsp/2½ US tsp dried yeast
200 ml/7 fl oz/¾ cup warm water
1½ tbsp/1¾ US tbsp olive oil
115 g/4 oz/¾ cup black olives, halved and stoned
115 g/4 oz/¾ cup sun-dried tomatoes
1 tsp/1¼ US tsp sea salt

to brush: *1 tbsp/1¼ US tbsp olive oil*

♣

Place flour and salt in a bowl. Sprinkle in the yeast and mix well. Pour in the warm water and olive oil and mix to a dough – use a bit more water if the dough is too dry. Turn dough out onto a lightly-floured surface and knead for about 10 minutes. When the dough has reached an elastic consistency, put into a clean bowl. Cover with clingfilm/Saran wrap and leave in a warm place – ideally on a baking rack on top of warming plate on an Aga or an airing cupboard. The aim is for it to double in size, which will take approximately 1½ hours. After the dough has risen, turn out onto flat surface and knead it again for 3 minutes. Form it into an oblong shape and place onto an oiled baking sheet. Chop up tomatoes and mix with olives. Brush dough with olive oil and sprinkle the tomatoes and olives on top. Cover with a damp tea towel/dish cloth and leave the dough to rise again for a further 25 minutes. Bake at 190°C/375°F/gas 5 for about 30 minutes or until cooked in centre and golden-edged. Cut into squares and serve warm.

A classical Georgian mansion made of fine sandstone and built by Charles Lanyon in
1836 for the McCausland family, Drenagh commands impressive views of the
Sperrins and Donegal mountains. The gardens and woods which surround the
house are filled with rare and ancient trees and shrubs, and the paths which wind
through the glen provide delightful rambles for nature lovers. Cuisine at Drenagh is
based upon seasonal ingredients, making the most of local fish and game and using
fresh vegetables and herbs from the garden.

DRENAGH
LIMAVADY
Co DERRY
BT49 OHP

LIMAVADY 22649

EGGS WITH COD'S ROE SAUCE

4 eggs
4 slices brown bread
butter
4 slices smoked salmon

to garnish: *paprika, watercress/lettuce*

Cod's Roe Sauce
170 g/6 oz/⅔ cup smoked cod's roe
1 clove garlic
juice of 2 lemons
170 ml/6 fl oz/¾ cup olive oil
140 ml/5 fl oz/generous ½ cup single cream
salt and freshly-ground black pepper

♣

Put cod's roe and garlic in food processor. Slowly add the juice of half a lemon. Add oil slowly and the remainder of the lemon juice. Add cream and season with salt and freshly-ground black pepper.

To cook the eggs, place in boiling water for 5 minutes. Then soak in cold water and peel off shells.

Take crusts off bread and spread with butter. Put a slice of smoked salmon on each slice of bread. Place egg in centre of smoked salmon. Pour sauce over egg and sprinkle with paprika. Garnish with watercress or finely-sliced lettuce.

Anne Welch.

LEEKIE PUDDINGS WITH SPINACH SAUCE

4 medium-sized leeks
425 ml/¾ pint/2 cups milk
1 tbsp/1¼ US tbsp butter

Béchamel Sauce
1½ tbsp/1¾ US tbsp butter
1½ tbsp/1¾ US tbsp flour
milk reserved from cooking leeks
salt and freshly-ground pepper
fresh nutmeg
2 eggs, beaten

Spinach Sauce
450 g/1 lb cooked spinach or 1 packet (450 g/1 lb) frozen spinach
140 ml/¼ pint/⅔ cup cream
140 ml/¼ pint/⅔ cup plain yogurt

Roughly chop leeks and sauté lightly in butter. Add milk and simmer until soft. Strain leeks and reserve milk.

For the Béchamel sauce, make a roux with the butter and flour. Add milk from leeks and cook gently, stirring continuously, until thick and creamy. Season with salt, freshly-ground black pepper and a grating of fresh nutmeg. Cool slightly and then add beaten eggs. Lastly fold in the chopped leeks. Butter 4 ramekin dishes and spoon in the mixture. Place in a shallow oven dish in a *bain-marie*[*]. Bake in a pre-heated oven (180°C/350°F/gas 4) for 15 minutes or until set and risen. Remove from *bain-marie* and allow to cool slightly before turning out onto individual plates. Run a knife around the edge of the moulds to ease the puddings out.

To make spinach sauce, place spinach, cream and yogurt in liquidiser and blend until smooth. Season with salt and freshly-ground black pepper. Just before serving, heat *very* gently until lukewarm. On no account allow the sauce to boil. Pour the spinach sauce over and around the leekie puddings and serve.

[*]*Bain-marie*: a large deep tray filled with hot water into which dishes requiring slow cooking in the oven are placed; also used for keeping soups and sauces warm.

DRENAGH PHEASANT

2 young pheasants
115 g/4 oz/½ cup smoked bacon, diced
115 g/4 oz/1 stick butter
2 onions
1 clove garlic, crushed
2 tbsp/2½ US tbsp Armagnac or Calvados
115 ml/4 fl oz/½ cup white wine
425 ml/¾ pint/2 cups water
bay leaf, thyme and parsley

to sprinkle
115 g/4 oz streaky bacon
115 g/4 oz/1 cup fresh white breadcrumbs

Roux Base
2 tbsp/2½ US tbsp flour
2 egg yolks
140 ml/¼ pint/⅔ cup double cream

♣

Melt half the butter in a heavy casserole, add diced bacon and cook for 5 minutes. Add 1 sliced onion and the garlic. Cook gently until transparent. Remove onions and bacon from casserole and reserve.

Sauté pheasants in the casserole dish, adding more butter if necessary. Allow them to take colour gently. Flame with Armagnac or Calvados, then let it bubble and reduce slightly.

Return bacon and onions to casserole and add water, bay leaf, sprig of thyme and parsley. Turn heat low, cover and cook gently for about 45 minutes, turning birds over at half time.

While birds are cooking, chop bacon finely and fry until crisp. Add breadcrumbs and stir until brown, adding more butter if necessary. Reserve.

Remove pheasants from casserole, roughly shred meat and discard bones and skin. Place on a flat ovenproof dish and keep warm.

Chop remaining onion and cook in remaining butter, stir in flour. Strain stock from pheasants. Slowly add 425 ml/¾ pint/1⅔ cups of stock to the onion mixture. Cook for 5 minutes and then strain, pressing onion hard against side of sieve. Reduce and skim, adding more stock as you do so – the sauce should be syrupy. Mix beaten egg yolks with cream. Add a little of the hot sauce, then pour back into rest of sauce. Do not allow to boil. Sprinkle with breadcrumb and bacon mixture, place under grill/broiler until browned. Serve with a purée of celeriac and spiced red cabbage.

In Irish, Drimcong is *drom conga* – a narrow stretch of land between two lakes. The
history of the present house dates back to the seventeenth century when Isidore
Lynch was granted the house and demesne of Drimcong. It remained in the Lynch
family until 1804 when it passed over to Patrick Kilkelly whose descendants lived
there until the 1940s. During the 1960s and 1970s, Drimcong survived the
vicissitudes of changing fortunes under various owners until, in 1984, it was bought
by the renowned Irish chef Gerry Galvin and his wife Marie. Drimcong is now both
a family home and a well-known restaurant which is considered one of the
best in Ireland.

LOBSTER AND CHICKEN SAUSAGE

450 g/1 lb lobster meat, fresh from the cooked shell
450 g/l lb chicken breast, uncooked and skinned
carrot and leek, finely chopped (a generous tbsp of each)
115 g/4 oz fresh spinach
1 egg white
200 ml/7 fl oz/generous ⅔ cup cream
cayenne pepper
salt

Boil the carrot and leek in salted water for a minute. Remove vegetables with a slotted spoon and set aside to cool. In the same water, boil the spinach for a minute. Strain, cool and dry on clean kitchen paper. Chop chicken into 2½ cm/1" pieces and process with the egg white in a magimix or equivalent for 2 minutes. Remove chicken mixture from processor and put into a bowl which has been placed on a bed of iced water. Whisk cream into the chicken until completely incorporated. Chop the lobster into ½ cm/¼" pieces and combine well with the chicken and vegetables. Season with cayenne pepper and salt. Mould the mixture into portion-size sausages with cling film or foil. Remove these when shaped. Poach until slightly springy to the touch, about 10-12 minutes. Cool and reheat with butter in a frying pan. Serve with salad and lemon aïoli (page 82).

DRIMCONG HOUSE RESTAURANT MOYCULLEN GALWAY TELEPHONE 091 85115

LEMON AÏOLI

2 egg yolks
4 garlic cloves, crushed
1 tbsp/1¼ US tbsp fresh white breadcrumbs
juice of 1 lemon
300 ml/10 fl oz/1¼ cups olive oil
salt and ground white pepper

In a liquidiser, blend all the ingredients except the oil, salt and pepper.
Continue blending, adding the oil gradually. If the finished aïoli is too thick,
thin it with stock or a little water. Season to taste before serving.

GRILLED OYSTERS WITH GARLIC BUTTER

16 oysters
16 'coins' of garlic butter

Garlic Butter
225 g/8 oz/2 sticks softened butter
4 garlic cloves, peeled, blanched and crushed finely
2 tsp/2½ US tsp chopped parsley
salt, white pepper and lemon juice to taste

In a food processor, mix together the softened butter, garlic and parsley.
Season with salt, pepper and lemon juice. Make a roll of the finished butter
and wrap in foil or greaseproof/waxed paper. Refrigerate until required.
Pre-heat grill/broiler to its hottest. Open oysters (your fishmonger can do it
for you if you can't), detach muscles and leave oysters in their shells. Put
large coin shapes of garlic butter on top of each one and grill/broil until
bubbling. Serve with fresh brown soda bread.

RAGOUT OF WILD RABBIT
IN A CHOCOLATE-TEMPERED SAUCE

2 medium-sized rabbits
olive oil to sear
4 medium-sized carrots, peeled and sliced
3 sticks celery, sliced
3 cloves garlic, crushed
2 medium onions, sliced
280 ml/½ pint/1¼ cups red wine
1.1 L/2 pints/5 cups water or chicken stock
1 tbsp/1¼ US tbsp tomato purée
bouquet garni
lovage, parsley, rosemary and fennel
55 g/2 oz/2 squares dark chocolate, cut into 6 sections

Steep the skinned rabbits in a gallon of water with 280 ml/½ pint/1¼ cups
vinegar to clear them of blood. Dry and cut the rabbit into pieces – 8 legs
and 8 body cuts. Sear the meat in olive oil in a deep baking dish or roasting
tin until light brown, then strain off fat. Add vegetables and cook on top of
the cooker for 3 minutes. Add wine, water or stock, tomato purée and
reboil. Add herbs, cover with foil and bake for 90 minutes at
190°C/375°F/gas 5. Remove rabbit from cooking liquid and keep warm.
Strain liquid and discard vegetables and herbs. Reduce cooking liquid to a
pouring consistency and whisk in the chocolate little by little. Season if
necessary. Serve on a bed of cabbage and couscous/pasta, pouring the
sauce on top.

Set between the mountains and the sea in Ardmore, County Waterford, Dysert has
been the home of novelist Molly Keane for more than thirty years. She modified this
villa to 'sit like a cup in its saucer' using the services of a local carpenter, the late
Jack O'Brien. He laid flagstones, a square courtyard around the house and a simple
staircase to the road made from the copingstones of a ruined house. Inside, a solid
wooden half-door replaced a glass porch, and space was created for an ample
dining room and an enormous playroom for her children. The iron fireplaces, with
hobs to either side, became centrepoints to the warm, comfortable rooms.

SAWDUST EGGS

The originator of sawdust eggs was an old French/Irish lady who lived at
Pau and played golf with Edward VII. She loved to draw attention to a
brooch she always wore – crossed gold golf clubs with *very* small pearls
as balls. She always said, with reverence, 'My King gave me this'.
Perhaps sawdust eggs followed the round of golf.

a bunch of parsley
a bunch of chives
eggs as required
mayonnaise
Worcestershire sauce
anchovy sauce

♣

Snip a bunch of dry parsley and a few chives very finely. Press them
between two cloths to remove any dampness. Hard boil the required
number of eggs. When cold, remove shells without damaging whites and
dry whites completely. Slice a very small piece of white from the long side
of each egg, so that it can stand without wobbling. Cut each egg in half
lengthways. Stand both halves on a flat surface. Remove yolks and put them
through a sieve. Don't let them get pasty; keep them dry and fluffy. Mix in
parsley and chives. Fill both halves of each white with the egg-parsley-chive
mix. Don't press down. Put the stuffed halves together to form egg shapes
and place each in a small entrée dish. Leave in a cool place until needed.
Just before serving, cover each egg with a previously prepared thick
mayonnaise to which you have added a touch of anchovy sauce and
Worcestershire sauce. Sprinkle lightly with the remaining egg-parsley mix.
Serve eggs alongside a dish of very good *hors d'oeuvre* which should
include smoked trout, tomato salad and peppers.

MARY-BRIGID'S MERINGUES

Mary-Brigid had heard a rumour that some people used hot whiskey,
preferably Irish, instead of hot spring water (always 'spring water',
no matter which tap it ran from) but she never tried it. I have and it is
very good.

Makes 1 dozen meringues

2 egg whites
175 g/6 oz/¾ cup caster (superfine) sugar
175 ml/6 fl oz/¾ cup double (heavy) cream, lightly whipped

♣

Heat the oven to 70°C/150°F/gas 1. Cover a baking sheet with well-greased
greaseproof/waxed paper. Put the egg whites into a large bowl, add
1½ tbsp of boiling water and whisk until very stiff. Whisk in half the sugar
until thick, then gently fold in the remaining sugar. Spoon out onto the
baking sheet and cook for at least 2½ hours until dry and crisp. Remove
from the baking sheet with a palette knife and put the meringues upside-
down on a clean, ungreased baking tin. Return this to the oven and
continue to dry them out at the lowest possible heat until all traces of sticky
bottoms have vanished.

For a whole meringue pudding, use the same quantities of egg white
and sugar, adding a small teaspoon of instant coffee to the hot water. When
beaten, divide the mixture onto the backs of two sandwich tins lined with
two thicknesses of well-greased greaseproof/waxed paper. Cook at the
same heat but for rather longer (touching the tops with a finger will tell you
how firm the meringue is). Remove from the oven and strip off the paper
while the meringue is still hot. Return to the oven at a low heat and dry out.
When cool, or the next day, place ½ meringue on a plate, cover with softly
whipped cream and put the other half on top. Leave in the refrigerator for
1-2 hours and serve immediately (the refrigerator has some obscure action
that leaves the meringue crumbly, not hard and sticky).

FRIED POTATO PEEL

washed peel from 3 large potatoes
approx 100 g/4 oz/1 cup plain flour
salt and freshly-ground black pepper
oil for deep frying

Mix the flour, salt and pepper together, then add sufficient water to make a stiff batter. Coat the potato peelings in the batter. Fill a deep-fat frying pan ⅓ full of oil and heat to 190°C/375°F or until hot and smoking. Fry the peels in batches until crisp.

Grange Lodge is an ivy-clad Georgian house set in nearly twenty acres of land. Parts of the house date back to the late seventeenth century. In the early 1900s it was the home of Senator Stevenson whose family were connected to Moygashel Irish linen. The present owners, Ralph and Norah Brown, have run it successfully as a country house for visitors for many years and their hospitality has earned them many awards.

Grange Lodge
Dungannon

Moy (08687) 84512
or (08687) 22458

APPLE POTATO CAKE

450 g/1 lb freshly-boiled potatoes
115 g/4 oz/1 cup plain flour
1 tsp/1¼ US tsp salt
15 g/½ oz/¼ stick butter

Apple Filling
450 g/1 lb Armagh Bramley apples, peeled, cored and chopped
sugar to taste
knob of butter

Mash potatoes, salt and butter and work in flour. Divide in 2 halves and roll into rounds. Place apple filling on one round, keeping 2 cm/1" from the edge. Top with other round and seal well, trimming from the edges. Cook on both sides on a well-heated griddle or heavy-based frying pan for 10 minutes each side.

To serve, cool slightly and cut into 4 sections. Serve with thick grilled sausages, bacon and mushrooms. A delicious breakfast treat.

WILSON'S MURPHYS
IN A CLOGHER VALLEY SMOKY MIST

4 medium potatoes, scrubbed
4 tbsp/5 US tbsp fresh cream
85 g/3 oz smoked bacon, chopped
55 g/2 oz/½ cup smoked cheese, grated
black pepper and salt to taste

Boil potatoes until cooked but still holding their shape. Strain, cool slightly and cut into wedges. Place wedges in a buttered ovenproof dish and sprinkle with cream, bacon and cheese. Season to taste. Bake for 20-25 minutes at 200 C/ 400 F/gas 6 until crisp.

BUSHMILLS PORRIDGE

1 cup white speedicook oat flakes
3 cups cold water
1 tsp/1¼ US tsp salt

♣

Put all the ingredients in a cast iron pot with lid and place in bottom oven of two-oven Aga overnight. Alternatively, place in covered saucepan, bring to the boil and simmer for 10 minutes.

Divide into 4 bowls, pour 1 tbsp/1¼ US tbsp 10 year old Bushmills Malt Whiskey around the edge until the porridge almost floats. Sprinkle with brown sugar, and add fresh cream, according to taste. Guaranteed to help you face any frosty morning!

SULTANA SODA BREAD OR SPOTTED DICK

3 cups soda bread flour
or
Alternatively, add
1 tsp/1¼ US tsp baking soda
1 tsp/1¼ US tsp cream tartar
1 tsp/1¼ US tsp salt
to 3 cups plain flour

170 g/6 oz/1¼ cups sultanas/raisins
425 ml/¾ pint/1⅔ cups buttermilk

Sieve/sift all dry ingredients into a bowl. Add sultanas/raisins and stir in buttermilk. Mix well and pour into a well-greased 1 kg/2 lb loaf tin. Bake for 30 minutes at 200°C/400°F/gas 6. Reduce heat to 150°C/300°F/gas 2 for a further 20-25 minutes. Turn onto a cooling tray.

Serve sliced with butter and jam. Delicious toasted or fried the following day – if there's any left!

Built before the turn of the century, Gubbeen House has been the home of the
Ferguson family for five generations. Set in trees one mile from Schull in West Cork,
it faces the Atlantic and Fastnet Lighthouse, with Mount Gabriel behind it. Gubbeen
has given its name to an award-winning semi-soft cheese made from the milk of the
Fergusons' own herd of Friesian and Jersey cows. Giana Ferguson is a superb cook
and grew up in what she calls 'a kitchen culture'. Her father was a wine merchant
for a time and her grandfather was the famous epicure and ambassador, Sir Harry
Luke, author of *The Tenth Muse*, a gourmet's compendium.

GUBBEEN CHEESE

Gubbeen House, Schull, County Cork. Ireland
Telephone: 028 · 28231 · Fax 028 · 28573

ROSARIO'S CALDO VERDE

This is a Spanish soup version of the traditional Irish colcannon.

225 g/½ lb dark green cabbage – Savoy or Greyhound
450 g/1 lb potatoes
115 g/4 oz coarse garlic sausage (preferably smoked and firm-textured)
½ cup of a very fine-quality olive oil (Spanish or Portuguese is best, with
strong olive flavours)
salt and pepper

♣

Using the dark green leaves of the cabbage, roll them cigarwise into tight bundles. Shave them into layers and put them into a bowl of cold water. Peel and chunk the potatoes. Put them to boil in approximately 1.4 L/ 2½ pints/6 cups of lightly-salted water. Cook until soft.

Cut the sausage into 1¼ cm/½" chunks and cook slowly in simmering water for 20 minutes.

Once the potatoes are soft, lift them out of the water and press them back into their own water through either a sieve or a foodmill. Bring the potato soup back to a gentle boil, then add the olive oil and salt and pepper to taste.

Drain the greens (which should look like permed hair) and add to the potato soup and simmer for 6-8 minutes.

Serve with the drained sausage floating on top.

CROOKHAVEN CLAM CHOWDER

At Easter, on several beaches around Crookhaven, you can find fresh clams.
You need a bucket, a strong rake, a pair of wellies and a hip flask. Allow
about 12 clams per person. If there is time, it is a good rule to soak the
clams for several hours in water with a handful of porridge oats
to clean them out.

36-48 fresh clams
4 scallops
225 g/½ lb monkfish
juice of 1 lemon

Chowder Stock
4 large potatoes
30 g/1 oz/¼ stick butter
1 onion
2 sticks celery
1 tsp fresh thyme
1 level tbsp/1¼ US tbsp flour
570 ml/1 pint/2½ cups milk
280 ml/½ pint/1¼ cups fish stock
1 bay leaf

to garnish: *garlic croûtons*

♣

Peel and dice the potatoes and leave in water.

Melt half the butter in a large heavy pan. Add the thinly-diced onions
and celery and sweat them until transparent. Add the thyme, then the flour,
and make a roux by slowly adding the milk.

Take the scallops from their shells, remove their beards and run your
thumb down the black vein to clean it out. Wash them under running
water, sprinkle them with the lemon juice and allow to stand for a few
minutes. Skin and cut the monkfish into generous lumps. In a skillet, seal
the monkfish and scallops in the rest of the butter.

Drain the potatoes and add them to the roux. Bring it back to a rolling
boil for about 10 minutes while you make the croutons.

Add the clams and the monkfish to the roux, then the potatoes. Add
salt to taste and a good amount of freshly-ground black pepper. Add the
bay leaf and return the mixture to a slow, rolling boil, stirring in the fish
stock to loosen it all. Stir it carefully until the potatoes are soft but not a
pulp.

Serve with very crunchy oven-dried garlic croûtons.

GUBBEEN GAME PÂTÉ

1 pheasant
1 good glass of sherry
225 g/½ lb lean pork
340 g/¾ lb rabbit meat or veal or chicken (depending on availability)
115 g/4 oz fatty rashers/bacon slices (green/unsmoked)
1 onion
55 g/2 oz/½ cup capers
1 tbsp/1¼ US tbsp juniper berries
1 tbsp/1¼ US tbsp black peppercorns, crushed
salt
3 bay leaves
sprig of fresh thyme

to garnish: *gelatine*

Bone the pheasant and trim the meat into natural fillets. Marinate the fillets for 6 hours, overnight if possible, in the sherry, slices of half the onion, a bay leaf and half the crushed peppercorns.

Make a stock of the pheasant bones using the other half of the onion, the rest of the crushed peppercorns, a bay leaf and the thyme, reducing it down over several hours to about 280 ml/½ pint/1¼ cups.

The next day, chop finely or mince/grind the lean pork with the other meat or game you are using.

Crush the juniper berries with a pestle and mortar and pound them into the minced meats, adding a good amount of salt and freshly-ground pepper. Add the stock by judging the dryness of the meat – it should be juicy, not swimming.

In a deep, thick earthenware terrine or dish lined with half the rashers/bacon slices, several juniper berries and a sprig of thyme or bay leaf, start layering – first the minced meats, then the drained fillets of pheasant, then some capers. Repeat this until you have used up the ingredients, finishing with the mince mixture. Place the remaining rashers/bacon slices on top and cover with a lid or several layers of tin foil.

Stand the terrine in a baking dish of hot water, half-way up the terrine, and cook in a moderate oven (180°C/350°F/gas 4) for 2 hours. Once cooked, the meats will have shrunk away from the dish walls, so allow it to cool down with a weight on top of it.

The remaining stock and the drained sherry marinade can be reduced and a little gelatine added. This can be used as a garnish once cooled and chopped around the terrine. Serve with hot fresh bread.

Set in 150 acres of private forest, Gurthalougha House is an early nineteenth century house overlooking the River Shannon on Lough Derg with spectacular views of the mountains of Clare and Galway. It was originally a hunting lodge belonging to the Farrar family whose remains are buried in an adjoining crypt. The house lies at the end of a long, winding avenue planted with walnut trees and is built around a cobbled courtyard which is always filled with flowers. Michael and Bessie Wilkinson who have run it as a country house for ten years have a long association with good food; Bessie's father was the famous Ken Besson who ran both the Russell and Hibernian Hotels in Dublin.

Tel.: 067-22080
Fax: 067-22154

Gurthalougha House,
Ballinderry,
Nenagh,
Co. Tipperary,
Ireland.

MARINATED SMOKED EEL

2 smoked eels, skinned, filleted and sliced lengthways
2 medium-sized onions (red ones give added colour)
115 ml/4 fl oz/½ cup red wine vinegar
280 ml/8 fl oz/1 cup sunflower oil
1 dsp/1½ US tbsp brown sugar
2 bay leaves
1 tsp/1¼ US tsp mustard powder
2 tsp/2½ US tsp crushed coriander seeds
black pepper, freshly-milled

♣

Layer finely-sliced onions and prepared smoked eel in a heavy crockery
pot. Add the bay leaves. Mix together all the other ingredients separately
and pour over the layered eel. Cover with cling film/Saran wrap and keep
in fridge. Best after 2-3 days. Serve on a bed of chopped lettuce.
(Note: Because eel is oily, olive oil is too heavy, so be sure to use the much
lighter sunflower oil.)

EGG NOODLES WITH AVOCADO AND SMOKED TROUT

egg noodles for 4
1 avocado, peeled and cubed
1 smoked trout fillet, flaked
280 ml/½ pint/1¼ cups cream
1 tbsp/1¼ US tbsp lemon juice
white pepper

to garnish: *parsley and fennel*

Plunge egg noodles into salted, boiling water and simmer for 5 minutes, until soft. Put all other ingredients in saucepan and heat. Pour the sauce over egg noodles and dust with chopped parsley and sprig of fennel before serving.

QUICK WHOLEMEAL SCONES

225 g/½ lb/2 cups wholemeal flour
225 g/½ lb/2 cups plain flour
1 tbsp/1¼ US tbsp butter
1 tsp/1¼ US tsp bread (baking) soda
350 ml/12 fl oz/1½ cups buttermilk

Place flours, butter and bread soda in a food processor. Blend and stop. Add buttermilk and blend until just mixed. Turn out on floured board and roll out lightly. Do not knead. Shape and cook for 20 minutes at 200°C/400°F/gas 6.

BREAST OF CHICKEN
WITH SMOKED TROUT AND CREAM CHEESE STUFFING

4 chicken breast fillets

Stuffing
115 g/4 oz/1 small packet cream cheese
115 g/4 oz/½ cup smoked trout
1 egg yolk
white pepper
dust of cayenne pepper
squeeze of lemon juice
1 dsp/1½ US tbsp parsley, chopped

Sauce
90 ml/3 fl oz/¼ cup white wine
115 ml/4 fl oz/½ cup cream

to garnish: *1 dsp/1½ US tbsp chopped chives*

♣

Flatten chicken breasts with a rolling pin. Mix stuffing ingredients in a bowl with a fork. Stuff chicken breasts and bake, covered with tin foil, for about 45 minutes at 180°C/350°F/gas 4. Remove to dish and keep warm. Heat the wine in the pan with the baking juices. Bring to the boil, add cream and reduce to thicken. Then pour over the chicken breasts. Garnish with chopped chives.

Black and silver falcons adorn the impressive entrance gates to Hilton Park, an imposing late Georgian mansion which has been home to the Madden family since 1734. Bought by Samuel Madden, a kinsman of Oliver Goldsmith, the house has a long and illustrious history. Set in the middle of rolling parkland and pastures, it is now owned by Johnny and Lucy Madden who run it as a country house. Lucy takes particular pride in her cooking which makes the most of the raw materials from her organic walled garden and is based on a philosophy that healthy eating can be both exciting to the palate and visually pleasing.

HILTON PARK
CLONES
CO. MONAGHAN
TELEPHONE: (047) 56007
FAX: (047) 56033

MELONS WITH SWEET CICELY

Sweet cicely is a perennial plant with vivid green leaves which impart a
most delicate flavour.

1 watermelon
2 other varieties of melon
1 orange (optional)
sweet cicely

Peel the melons and cut into slices. They should provide plenty of their
own juices, but you can add the juice of an orange. No sugar should be
necessary. Cut the freshly-picked sweet cicely into tiny fronds and sprinkle
over the fruit. Allow to rest for a ½ hour before eating.

POTATO BRIOCHE WITH GINGER

700 g/1½ lb potatoes, peeled
700 g/1½ lb/6 cups plain flour
1 tsp/1¼ US tsp ginger
2 sachets (about 50 g) ready-to-use dried yeast
115 g/4 oz/1 stick butter
55 g/2 oz/2 tbsp caster sugar
2 eggs
1 tsp/1¼ US tsp salt
2 tbsp/2½ US tbsp water

to dust: *icing/confectionery sugar*

♣

Boil the potatoes and drain well. Put them through a sieve and allow to cool. In a large bowl, sieve the flour with the ginger and mix with the potato purée. (At this stage, you can put the mixture into a food processor which takes away all the hard work.) Sprinkle in the yeast and rub in the butter. Add the caster sugar, eggs, salt and water. Knead until a silky elasticity is achieved. Put in a clean bowl, cover with a clean cloth and allow to rise in a warm place until the mixture is doubled in size.

Punch down the mixture and knead again briefly. Put in a greased, round cake tin, and leave to prove again until the dough reaches the top of the tin.

Bake in a hot oven (220°C/425°F/gas 7) for about 40 minutes (watching the top doesn't burn – you may need to turn down the heat after 20 minutes or so). Turn out and when still warm, sprinkle with icing/confectionery sugar and eat.

DRIED APRICOT JAM WITH ALMONDS

Makes about 12 pots

900 g/2 lb good-quality dried apricots
3 L/6 pints/15 cups of water
3 kg/6½ lb granulated sugar
115 g/4 oz/⅔ cup dried almonds

Cut the apricots into quarters and pour over the boiling water. Leave for 1½ days. Warm the sugar, add it to the fruit and water mixture and bring to the boil, stirring all the time. Allow to boil for about 30 minutes or until just set. Halfway through the boiling, add the skinned almonds, cut in halves.

Bottle in the usual way. If the jam seems a little too thick, unorthodox as it may be, I sometimes stir in a few tablespoons of boiling water just before eating.

A rambling country house outside the village of Shanagarry in County Cork, Kinoith is an old name which comes from the Irish *cuin ait* or *cion ait*, the quiet or friendly place. A Regency house from the early 1800s, it was built by a Quaker family called Strangman who owned the Cherry Breweries in Waterford. When Wilson Strangman died, the house was inherited by Ivan Allen of Ballymaloe in 1966 and since then has been the home of his son, Tim. Tim's wife Darina runs a cookery school at Kinoith in a converted apple barn and is the author of many best-selling Irish cookery books as well as presenting her own television series.

Kinoith House Shanagarry, Midleton, County Cork

TIMMY'S BROWN SODA BREAD

Timmy has adapted my original recipe and now makes the very best soda bread. It took quite a bit of coaxing to extract this recipe from him! He really does put in the pepper.

450 g/1 lb/4 cups white flour
560 g/1¼ lb/5 cups brown wholemeal flour
55 g/2 oz/⅔ cup kibbled/coarse whole wheat
55 g/2 oz/4 tbsp granary flour
55 g/2 oz/4 tbsp oatmeal
3 twists black pepper
2 rounded tsp/10 g/2½ US tsp salt
2 rounded tsp/10 g/2½ US tsp bread (baking) soda, sieved/sifted
900 ml/1½ pints/3¾ cups buttermilk or sour milk

♣

First, pre-heat the oven to 230°C/450°F/gas 8.

Mix the dry ingredients together thoroughly. Make a well in the centre and add most of the buttermilk or sour milk. Working from the centre, mix with your hand and add more milk if necessary. The dough should be soft but not sticky. Turn out on a floured board and knead lightly, just enough to shape into a round. Flatten gently to about 5 cm/2". Put onto a baking sheet. Mark with a deep cross in the top of the loaf and bake in the hot oven for 15-20 minutes. Then reduce the heat to 200°C/400°F/gas 6 for approximately 20-25 minutes or until the bread is cooked and sounds hollow when tapped. Cool on a wire rack.

FLORENCE BOWE'S CRUMPETS

Makes about 15

Another great standby, these crumpets can be made in minutes. My children
make them and cook them directly on the cool plate of the Aga.
They are also the ideal solution if you've got nothing in the tin when a
friend drops in.

225 g/½ lb/1¾ cups white flour
¼ tsp salt
½ tsp/¾ US tsp bread/baking soda
1 tsp/1¼ US tsp Bextartar/cream of tartar
2 eggs, preferably free range
250 ml/8 fl oz/1 cup milk
55 g/2 oz/scant ¼ cup caster sugar
30 g/1 oz/¼ stick butter

♣

Sieve/sift the dry ingredients into a bowl and rub in the butter. Drop the
eggs into the centre, add a little of the milk and stir rapidly with a whisk,
allowing the flour to drop gradually in from the sides. When half the milk is
added, beat until air bubbles rise. Add the remainder of the milk and allow
to stand for 1 hour, if possible*. Drop a good dessertspoonful/US
tablespoon into a hottish pan and cook until bubbles appear on the top.
It usually takes a bit of trial and error to get the temperature right. Flip over
and cook until golden on the other side. Serve immediately with butter and
home-made jam or, better still, apple jelly.

*They are usually lighter if the batter is allowed to stand, but I've often cooked them
immediately with very acceptable results.

RUSTIC ROAST POTATOES

These roast spuds cook very quickly and have an irresistible
crusty skin.

6 large 'old' potatoes (Golden Wonder or Kerr's Pink)
olive oil or beef dripping
sea salt

Pre-heat the oven to 230°C/450°F/gas 8. Scrub the potatoes well, cut
lengthways into quarters or into thick rounds approximately 2 cm/¾".
Put into a roasting tin, drizzle with olive oil and toss so they are barely
coated with olive oil. Roast in a pre-heated oven for 15-20 minutes,
depending on size. Sprinkle with sea salt and serve.

APPLE AND SWEET GERANIUM JELLY

Makes 6-7 pots

2.7 kg/6 lb crab apples or Bramley seedlings
2.7 L/4¼ pints/12½ cups water
*6-8 large sweet geranium leaves (*Pelargonium graveolens*),*
plus extra as needed
2 lemons
sugar

Wash the apples and cut into quarters – no need to peel or core. Windfalls
may be used, but make sure to cut out the bruised parts. Put the apples in a
large saucepan with the geranium leaves, the water and the thinly-pared
rind of the lemons. Cook until the apples dissolve into a 'mush',
approximately ½ hour.

Turn the pulp into a jelly bag and allow to drip until all the juice has
been extracted – usually overnight. Measure the juice into a preserving pan.
Allow 450 g/1 lb sugar to each pint (600 ml/2½ cups) of juice. Heat the
sugar in a moderate oven (180°C/350°F/gas 4) for about 10 minutes.
Squeeze the lemons, strain the juice and add to the preserving pan. Add a
few more geranium leaves if the flavour is still very mild. Bring to the boil
and add the sugar. Stir over a gentle heat until the sugar is dissolved.
Increase the heat and boil rapidly, without stirring, for about 8-10 minutes.
Remove the geranium leaves. Skim, test for set and then pour the jelly into
sterilised jars, with a sweet geranium leaf in each jar. Cover and seal
immediately.

A modern country house completed in 1989, Long Lake was designed like a
compass around a central brass and teak staircase with panoramic views of Kenmare
Bay and the Beara Peninsula on all sides. Constructed of Wicklow granite with a
copper mansard roof, the house is surrounded with rhododendrons, hundreds of
trees and shrubs as well as a lake. Owner Thomas Staus, who trained in hotel
management in Frankfurt, decided to make Ireland both his home and his place of
business when he saw the site for the first time. On the Ring of Kerry, Long Lake is
now run as a hotel which is noted for its fine food.

HOT MACKEREL QUICHE

6 smoked mackerel fillets, skinned
butter
1 leek
4 peppers, red and yellow
4 eggs
100 ml/4 fl oz/½ cup milk
salt, pepper, nutmeg, caraway seeds, chilli powder, juice of 1 lemon
puff pastry or 1 quiche pastry

Cut leek and peppers into matchstick lengths and sweat them with some butter, salt and pepper and spices in a covered pan without letting them brown. When soft, remove the lid and let the moisture evaporate. Line four 10 cm/4" circular pie dishes with pastry dough to about ½ cm/⅕" thickness. Cut the mackerel fillets into bite-size pieces and arrange them on the pastry. Cover with leeks and peppers. Whip the eggs and milk and pour over the fish. Bake for 20-30 minutes in a pre-heated oven at 180°C/350°F/gas 4.

Thomas Staus

LONG LAKE   TAHILLA   POST KILLARNEY   COUNTY KERRY   TEL 064 45100

TAHILLA LAMB STEW

The idea is a stew incorporating colourful vegetables and served in a simple deep dish.

500 g/1¼ lb well-hung lamb shoulder
frying oil
600 g/1⅓ lb potatoes
600 g/1⅓ lb carrots
300 g/¾ lb celeriac or celery in pieces of date size (keep trimmings)
100 ml/4 fl oz/½ cup red wine with body and acidity
salt and pepper
2 bay leaves
tomato purée
1 tsp/1½ US tsp mild paprika
1 sprig of fresh rosemary and thyme
1 garlic clove
pinch of cinnamon and ginger

♣

Shape the peeled celeriac and carrots into pieces of date size (thick carrots, quartered lengthwise, cut every 3 cm/1", then carved to date shape.) The trimmings, around 200 g/7 oz, serve to thicken the stew. Shape the peeled potatoes the same way.

Cut the lamb meat to cubes of walnut size, discarding sinew and bones. Simmer the sinew and eventually extra bones in 1 L/2 pints/5 cups of water with a teaspoon of salt for a lamb stock.

Fry the lamb cubes in several goes, hot and brief, to seal and to brown well. Do not put too many pieces of meat into the pan at one time to avoid them boiling. Then remove them and fry the onions to a light brown colour. Add the carrot and celeriac trimmings. Add a tablespoon of tomato purée and stir. The tomato purée will quickly stick to the pot. Before it gets burned (and bitter), add the red wine and let it boil up. Then add the stock and the spices. Simmer until the meat is tender. In the meantime, boil the carrots, celeriac and potatoes.

Take the meat out and press the sauce through a sieve. Boil it down to a thick consistency. Put the meat back in to reheat and season to taste. Pour the stew into a serving dish and decorate it with vegetables sprinkled randomly over it.

WILD BLACKBERRY CRÈME WITH BLACKBERRY COULIS

250 g/9 oz/1½ cups fresh wild blackberries, puréed
150 ml/5 fl oz/⅔ cup yogurt
80 g/3 oz/3 tbsp sugar
the marrow of 2 vanilla pods
100 ml/4 fl oz/½ cup milk
2 egg yolks
1 x 11g (0.4 oz) sachet powdered gelatine
250 ml/½ pint/1¼ cups whipped cream

Blackberry Coulis
150 g/5½ oz/1¼ cups blackberries, puréed
sugar to taste
2 tbsp Cointreau

Boil the milk, vanilla and sugar in a metal bowl and stir in the egg yolks.
Place the bowl over a pot of boiling water. Keep stirring while on the steam
until this custard thickens. Then take it off, sprinkle on the gelatine and put
it aside until cooled to room temperature. Blend yogurt and blackberry
purée. Finally fold in the whipped cream. Fill it into wide open glasses, or
glass bowls. Chill for 6 hours and serve with the coulis.

Overlooking the Blackwater, one of the most beautiful river valleys in Ireland, Longueville was built in 1720. Two wings were added in 1800 and the Turner conservatory in 1862. Originally built on O'Callaghan land and confiscated during the time of Cromwell, the house returned to O'Callaghan ownership after some 300 years when Senator William O'Callaghan bought the Georgian mansion in 1938. Now run as a family hotel, it has the added distinction of being a registered vineyard, selling its own Chateau Longueville Cois Moire wine.

LONGUEVILLE ·HOUSE
& PRESIDENTS' RESTAURANT

Mallow Co. Cork
Republic of Ireland

Tel. (022) 47156/47306 Fax No. 022/47459

Avocado Mousse

3 or 4 avocados, nice and ripe
½ lemon
salt and pepper
1 dsp/1½ US tbsp olive oil

♣

Peel the avocados. Remove the stones and blend the flesh in the magimix or food processor until there are no lumps left. Season with salt, pepper, lemon juice and add olive oil. Mix again. Place mousse in a circular mould and chill until firm. When ready to serve, remove mousse from the mould and place on a serving dish. Garnish with an assortment of lettuces and garlic croûtons.

William O'Callaghan

Mussels with Herb Breadcrumbs
and an Aromatic Tomato Sauce

3 kg/7 lb mussels
½ onion
1 carrot
1 sprig of parsley
1 sprig of thyme
1 glass white wine
1 knob of butter

Herb Breadcrumbs
4 stale slices of bread, crumbed
1 sprig of thyme
2 tbsp/2½ US tbsp parsley, chopped
1 sprig of rosemary
1 sprig of fennel
1½ tbsp/1¾ US tbsp olive oil

Tomato Sauce
6 tomatoes
½ fennel
1 onion
1 sprig of thyme
1 star of anise

Wash all the dirt off the mussels, removing the beards. In a deep pot, sweat the vegetables and herbs. Then add in the mussels with the white wine and place a lid over them. Shake them occasionally and when all the shells have opened (in a few minutes), remove from heat. Strain off the mussels and reserve the stock. Remove the flesh from the shells and keep aside.

Blend the breadcrumbs with the herbs and olive oil.

For the tomato sauce, remove the seeds from the tomatoes. Sweat the chopped onion and fennel in a sauté pan. Add in the tomatoes, the star of anise and the mussel stock. Simmer for 15 minutes and then blend in a magimix or food processor. Place in a greased mould 4 cm/2" high and 5 cm/3" wide on a baking tray. Season the warm mussels and press into the mould, leaving some space for the breadcrumbs on the top. Place under a hot grill/broiler until well coloured. Unmould in the centre of a plate and surround with the sauce which has been seasoned to taste.

ESCALOPE OF BRILL WITH A MUSTARD GRAIN SAUCE

1 brill (about 1½-2 kg/3½-4 lbs)
1 dsp/1½ US tbsp dry mustard seed
1 glass white wine
4 shallots, peeled
10 fresh white mushrooms
45 g/1½ oz/⅓ stick butter
½ glass water
½ glass cream

The night before preparing, soak the mustard seeds in ¼ glass of white wine. Cut the brill into 4 fillets, removing the skin (or get your fishmonger to do this). Chop the shallots and slice the mushrooms and sauté lightly in 10 g/¼ oz/½ tbsp butter. Add the water and the remainder of the white wine. Place the fish fillets on top and cover with greaseproof/waxed paper. Place the pan in the oven at 150°C/300°F/gas 2 until fish is nearly cooked – about 10 minutes (observation is best). Remove the fillets and place on a plate, cover with paper towelling and leave in a warm area.

Strain the cooking liquid from the pan into a casserole (mushrooms and shallots are discarded). Reduce by a third, then add cream and reduce again for 5 minutes. Whisk in the remainder of the butter, which should be ice cold, and season to taste. Pat the fish fillets dry, place them on warmed plates and pour the sauce over them.

Luggala was originally built in the 1790s as a hunting lodge for the La Touche banking family. It has a fairytale setting on a 7000-acre deer and pheasant-filled estate overlooking Lough Tay in County Wicklow. With its little battlements, turrets and quatrefoil windows, this white 'wedding cake house' is almost dwarfed by its backdrop of immense, mature trees. The original house, constructed around a cobbled inner courtyard, was completely destroyed by a fire in 1956 and an exact replica was then rebuilt. It was given to the present owner, the Honourable Garech de Brún, by his mother Oonagh, Lady Oranmore and Browne, the daughter of Ernest Guinness. When Garech de Brún married Princess Purna of Morvi, the cooking at Luggala became a combination of Irish and Indian cuisine.

log á lága,
An Tócap,
Conndae Cill Manntáin.

Bengali Fish with Mustard Seed

Serve with drinks as an appetiser, or as a first course.

900 g/2 lb cod or other firm white fish, cubed into 3¾ cm/1½ " pieces
1½ tsp/1¾ US tsp mustard seed, crushed
1 lime, squeezed
4 tbsp/5 US tbsp mustard oil
sea salt to taste
3 to 6 green chillies, according to taste

to serve: *lime wedges*

Marinate the cod in the crushed mustard seed, lime juice, mustard oil and sea salt. Leave for 10 minutes. Score chillies once with a knife lengthways. Put a bit more mustard oil into a frying pan and add the chillies, followed by the cod which should be cooked for 3 minutes each side. The chillies may be discarded. Serve with lime wedges.

MEM SAHEB'S SHEPHERD'S PIE

This is usually called Mem Saheb's Eshepherd's Pie in India. All mountainy lamb closely resembles Indian lamb and its diet is similarly uncontaminated. Kid is often used in India for this dish.

900 g/2 lb minced/ground Wicklow Lamb, bones reserved for stock
2 tbsp/2½ US tbsp olive oil
1 tbsp/1¼ US tbsp butter
1½ Spanish onions, chopped
2 garlic cloves, smashed and finely chopped
6 medium-sized carrots, minced/ground
3 tomatoes, finely chopped
1½ tbsp/1¾ US tbsp Italian tomato concentrate
or 1 tin Italian tomatoes, chopped, with their juice
1 small piece fresh ginger, minced/ground
1 tbsp/1½ US tbsp each of freshly-chopped thyme, bay leaf, sage
½ tsp ground coriander
½ tsp ground cinnamon
¼ tsp black pepper, freshly-ground
1 tbsp/1¼ US tbsp Worcestershire sauce
1 tbsp/1¼ US tbsp Japanese soya sauce, in lieu of salt
tabasco to taste
lamb stock
4 large boiled potatoes
1 egg, beaten

♣

Sweat the chopped onions, followed by the garlic, in olive oil and butter until transparent. Add the minced lamb and sauté, stirring continuously until brown. Stir in the minced carrots, tomatoes and ginger and add the spices and finely-chopped herbs. Cover with lamb stock. Season with Worcestershire sauce, soya sauce, tabasco and freshly-ground black pepper. Simmer for 30 to 40 minutes until meat is tender. Pour off surplus fat and place the mixture in a well-buttered, deep oval pie dish.

Mash cooked potatoes with the beaten egg. Season to taste with butter and freshly-ground black pepper. Cover the meat with the mashed potato and brown in the oven for 8 to 10 minutes or until golden (200°C/400°F/gas 6). Serve with Worcestershire sauce.

LOUISE O'MORPHY'S VENISON CHOPS

The Japanese Sika Deer has become naturalised in the Wicklow Mountains, having escaped from the Deer Park in the Powerscourt Demesne. Louis XVth's mistress, Louise O'Morphy, was made famous in Boucher's portrait which showed her recumbent naked back view in La Salle des Menus Plaisirs at Versailles. She also lived in Le Parc aux Cerfs (The Deer Park) from which she too escaped. The house was originally built by the Royal Huntsman, Louis XIII.

8 or 12 Wicklow Sika venison chops
3 tbsp/3¾ US tbsp olive oil
1 tbsp/1¼ US tbsp butter
freshly-ground black pepper

The Marinade
½ bottle red burgundy
1 tbsp/1¼ US tbsp freshly-ground black pepper
12 juniper berries
3 cloves
3 bay leaves
4 tbsp/5 US tbsp mixed herbs
2 tbsp/2½ US tbsp soya sauce
4 tbsp/5 US tbsp Italian tomato purée
2 tbsp/2½ US tbsp Dijon mustard
6 tbsp/7½ US tbsp redcurrant jelly
3 tbsp/3¾ US tbsp marmalade
2 tbsp/2½ US tbsp Worcestershire sauce
4 tbsp/5 US tbsp balsamic vinegar
juice of ½ lemon
1 cup brandy

Whisk together all the ingredients, except the brandy, for the marinade. Place the venison chops in the marinade for 2 days, turning them 4 times a day.

After removing the venison, strain the marinade and boil for 5 minutes. Then add the brandy and boil for 5 more minutes or until the sauce is syrupy.

Fry the chops in the olive oil, butter and freshly-ground black pepper for 3 to 5 minutes per side, according to taste. Serve at once.

No salt should be added as it shrinks and dries out venison.

Markree Castle, Sligo's oldest inhabited castle, has been the home of the Cooper
family since 1640. The original house was altered and rebuilt many times, with the
major external transformation carried out in 1802 by the well-known architect
Francis Johnston. The magnificent oak staircase is overlooked by a stained glass
window supposedly tracing the Cooper family tree back to King John of England.
Charles Cooper is the tenth generation of his family to live in Markree, which was
once described as Ireland's finest castle of its period. It is now run as a country
house hotel and boasts one of the most spectacular dining rooms in Ireland.

Chef: Tom Joyce

FILLET OF PORK WITH APPLE AND PORT SAUCE

2 large pork fillets
oil to seal
1 small onion, chopped
1 clove of garlic, crushed
1 glass of red wine
2 measures of port
1 tsp/1¼ US tsp sugar
300 ml/10 fl oz/1¼ cups cream
1 red apple
seasoning to taste

♣

Trim pork fillets and remove connective tissue. Season pork. Heat oil in pan and seal pork all over. Cook for 15 minutes. Remove excess oil and add chopped onion and garlic. Cook slightly. Add wine, port, sugar and cream. Allow to reduce by one third.

Cut some parisienne (small) balls from the red apple, leaving on skin. Chop remaining apple and add to the sauce. Remove fillets from pan and keep warm. Whisk sauce and strain into small pot. Slightly sauté the apple parisienne in butter and 1 tsp of water, then add to sauce.

To serve, slice pork fillet and fan onto plate. Thread with sauce and apple. Garnish with a tomato rose and fresh watercress.

TERRINE OF PHEASANT WITH ORANGE AND MANGO SAUCE

Terrine
1 pheasant
115 g/4 oz pork fat
1 measure of brandy
55 g/2 oz/1 cup white bread (croutons)
200 ml/7 fl oz/¾ cup cream
1 breast of chicken
2 egg whites
115 g/4 oz wild mushrooms
200 g/7 oz/1 cup fine-diced carrot, onion and celery
½ glass dry white wine
seasoning to taste

Orange and Mango Sauce
juice of 3 oranges
1 ripe mango, peeled and stoned
1 glass of white wine
55 g/2 oz/2 tbsp caster sugar

Debone the pheasant and dice flesh. Marinate pheasant and pork fat with brandy, half the cream, bread and seasoning. Refrigerate and marinate for 12 hours.

Cut chicken breast and purée in processor with remaining cream, 2 egg whites and seasoning. Refrigerate.

Sweat all vegetables and white wine together and reduce until liquid evaporates. Allow vegetables to cool. Bind the chicken mousse (purée) to the vegetables. Season with salt and freshly-ground pepper. Mince/grind the chilled marinade mixture and bind with 1 egg white. Place the mixture onto a double sheet of tin foil (not cling film) and spread out into a rectangle 5 cm x 5 cm/2" x 2". Spread the chicken mousse on top. Roll up and seal each end. Cook in a tray of water or stock for 45 minutes. Remove and allow to cool.

Combine all sauce ingredients in a blender and process until smooth. Chill and serve with the pheasant terrine.

Lemon Tart with Plum and Basil Coulis

Pastry
200 g/7 oz/2 cups flour
115 g/4 oz/1 stick butter or ½ cup margarine
55 g/2 oz/2 tbsp caster sugar
1 egg

Filling
4 eggs
150 g/5½ oz/⅔ cup caster sugar
175 ml/6 fl oz/⅔ cup cream
juice and zest of 2 lemons

Plum and Basil Coulis
4-5 ripe plums, sliced
55 g/2 oz/2 tbsp caster sugar
1 glass red wine
fresh basil

Make the sweet pastry by placing the flour, butter and sugar in a blender and mixing well. Add the egg to flour and mix. Knead to a smooth paste. Roll and line a 20 cm x 2½ cm/9" x 1" flan/pie ring and bake blind for 10 minutes at 180°C/350°F/gas 4. Then reduce the temperature to 150°C/300°F/gas 2.

Make the filling by placing all the ingredients into a liquidiser and mix. Then pour the mixture into the pastry case and cook for 20-25 minutes until the mixture is setting. Cool and refrigerate.

Make the coulis by liquidising the sliced plums, sugar and wine. Then pass through a fine sieve. Add the freshly-chopped basil and leave to infuse for at least 1 hour before use.

To serve, dust the slice of tart with icing/confectionery sugar and serve with the plum and basil coulis.

Surrounded by lawns and wooded parkland, Martinstown House was built in the
early years of the nineteenth century as a shooting lodge for the 2nd Duke of
Leinster. It is one of the few houses in Ireland attributed to the architect
Decimus Burton who laid out the gardens at Áras an Uachtaráin, the residence of
the President of Ireland. It is thought that he was employed to rebuild the house
for the Duke's mistress, a certain Miss Martin, who became known as the
'Hibernian Patriot'.

THE CURRAGH, CO. KILDARE
045-471269

CHEESE PUDDING

This first course or luncheon dish was given by
the late Mrs Richard Guinness.

55 g/2 oz/½ stick butter
55 g/2 oz/4 tbsp flour
salt and freshly-ground black pepper
280 ml/½ pint/1¼ cups milk
4 eggs, separated
85 g/3 oz/⅔ cup grated cheddar and Parmesan cheese, mixed total
280 ml/½ pint/1¼ cups cream

♣

Melt the butter and add the flour, seasonings and warmed milk to make a
thick Béchamel sauce. Let it cool and then add the yolks of 4 eggs. Beat
well and add cheeses. Finally, whip the egg whites very stiffly and fold into
the mixture. Pour into a buttered soufflé dish or pudding basin and steam
for 1½ hours. The pudding can remain in the steamer until required. Turn
out onto a fireproof dish. Cover with the cream, sprinkle with a little more
cheddar cheese and put under grill/broiler to brown. Delicious with green
salad and crusty bread.

Meryl Long.

ROAST BARBARY DUCK WITH BROWN ORANGE SAUCE

We are lucky to have a local farm that produces these huge dark-fleshed ducks. One duck weighing 2¾-3½ kg/6-8 lb feeds 4-5 easily. I rub the duck with sea salt and flour, prick it a little with a skewer and roast it, preferably on a rack, basting from time to time, for approximately 2 hours in a moderate oven (220°C/425°F/gas 7/top right-hand oven of Aga).

Sage and Onion Stuffing
4 slices of bread, made into crumbs
1 large onion, finely chopped and sweated in about 55 g/2 oz/
½ stick butter until soft and golden
plenty of chopped sage leaves
salt and black pepper, freshly ground

Mix all together and stuff the duck.

Brown Orange Sauce

This depends on a really good stock made by boiling up bones, carcasses, vegetables and herbs – if possible overnight in bottom right-hand oven of the Aga. Then fry 1 chopped onion and 2 thick rashers/slices of bacon in a little butter until brown. Add 30 g/1 oz/2 tbsp of flour and when well incorporated, add 570 ml/1 pint/2½ cups of good stock and 1 tsp of tomato purée, *bouquet garni*, salt and pepper and a few mushrooms, if available. Let all this simmer very gently for about 1 hour. Then put through a nylon sieve. Return to a clean saucepan and add 1 glass of red wine or port and the juice of a large orange. Finally, add the orange rind which has been cut into julienne strips and blanched for 5 minutes.

Roast potatoes are delicious cooked in the duck fat. We parboil them first and shake in the pan to rough up the outside. We usually serve an apple sauce to which we add a little lemon juice and a knob of butter.

Strawberries in Elderflower Syrup
with Tuiles d'Amandes

*450 g/1 lb strawberries (we grow the old-fashioned Royal Sovereign which
I think are the most delicious)*
85 g/3 oz/3 tbsp golden granulated sugar (ordinary will do)
1 lemon, juice and finely-pared rind
300 ml/½ pint/1¼ cups water
2 handfuls of elderflowers

Put the sugar and lemon rind into the water. When the sugar has dissolved,
boil quickly for 4-5 minutes. Take the pan from the heat and add the lemon
juice and elderflowers. Let this cool completely to absorb flavour, then
strain it through a nylon sieve. It can then be poured over the hulled
strawberries.

Tuiles d'Amandes
(very thin, curled biscuits)
2 egg whites
115 g/4 oz/½ cup caster sugar
(we flavour it with vanilla pods in storage jars)
55 g/2 oz/4 tbsp flour, sieved/sifted
30 g/1 oz/¼ cup almonds, blanched and flaked
55 g/2 oz/½ stick unsalted butter

Beat egg whites and sugar. Add flour, almonds and butter which has been
melted but not hot. Grease baking sheets (or use bakewell paper) and
spread out the mixture in teaspoons to make circles. Bake to a golden
brown in a moderate oven (180°C/350°F/gas 4). Then lift off carefully and
lay over the handle of a wooden spoon to cool. Store immediately in an
airtight tin. The biscuits should be very thin and slightly curled.

A baronial-style Victorian house with crenellations, Mount Falcon Castle was built in 1876 for a local landowner, John Frederick Knox, by the Kerry-born architect, Joseph Franklin Fuller, who also designed Ashford Castle. It was bought in 1932 by Colonel Bob Aldridge and his wife Connie who started to take in fishing friends as guests and gradually made hospitality their business. Since her husband's death in 1976, Connie has continued to run Mount Falcon in her own inimitable way.

Mount Falcon Castle

Telephone: (096) 21172.
Fax.: (096) 21172.

BALLINA,
Co. Mayo.

GRAVAD LAX

3.6 kg/8 lb salmon, cleaned and filleted, but not washed
6 tbsp/7½ US tbsp sugar
6 tbsp/7½ US tbsp salt
3 tbsp/3¾ US tbsp white pepper
good handful of fresh dill

♣

Sprinkle the sugar, salt and pepper mixture on a sheet of greaseproof/waxed paper. Add a layer of dill stalks. Press salt mixture onto the cut sides of both salmon fillets. Place one fillet on the greaseproof/waxed paper, skin side down. Cover this with plenty of dill. Place the next fillet, cut side down, on top. Sprinkle on the rest of the salt mixture. Cover with dill and wrap the fish up in the greaseproof/waxed paper. Then parcel it up in tin foil with a light weight on top and leave in a very cool place (but not the fridge) for 48 hours, turning the fish once. Carefully scrape off all the salt mixture and dill. Wipe the salmon carefully and slice thinly like smoked salmon. Serve with a dill sauce.

C. W. Aldridge.

JUGGED HARE

1 hare, cut off the bone (in large pieces). Reserve blood and liver.
850 ml/1½ pints/3¼ cups hare stock
2 rashers/slices streaky bacon
seasoned flour
butter for frying
thyme, bay leaf, parsley, cloves, peppercorns
2 tbsp marmalade
¾ bottle red wine
lemon juice
onions

Steep the hare pieces in a marinade of red wine, herbs and spices overnight. Boil up the bones for stock. Roll meat in the seasoned flour and brown in a little butter along with the onions and chopped bacon. Remove the meat, add flour to soak up any fat or add another little bit of butter. Then add stock and herbs, bring to the boil and stir for a few minutes. Pour this and the meat into a heavy casserole and boil for 2 hours on a slow heat until very tender. Add blood, mashed liver, red wine marinade, marmalade and lemon juice, if needed. Simmer for about 20 minutes. (I prefer wine and marmalade to port and redcurrant jelly.)

ROAST WOODCOCK

The woodcock shoots in County Mayo mostly comprise visitors from the Continent who are escaping to the West of Ireland and its winters which are much milder than those of mainland Europe.

The birds must be carefully plucked, head and all, because the entire bird is roasted, undrawn (not gutted). They are best if hung for 4-5 days.

Woodcock must not be cooked too quickly so that they remain juicy and slightly pink. Season well, then wrap a large rasher/slice of bacon around each bird. Skewer the rasher with the bird's long beak. Place each bird on a lightly buttered piece of bread to catch the juices during roasting.

Pre-heat the oven to 200°C/400°F/gas 6. Roast the birds for 20-25 minutes, then serve with a thin gravy which is made from the juices of the roasted birds. This can be enlivened with a squeeze of lemon and a dash of red wine.

Newbay House was built in 1822 for Henry Halton, a mayor of Wexford. In its
outbuildings, this late Georgian house incorporates a fourteenth-century castle and a
seventeenth-century farmhouse. In 1869, Thomas Jeffries added another wing and
carried out major alterations. Newbay is now owned by Paul and Mientje Drum who
run it as a country house which is open to guests.

Newbay Country House

WEXFORD, IRELAND
Telephone: 053 - 22779
Fax: 053 - 24318

LIVER TERRINE

450 g/1 lb pork liver
1 small tin anchovy fillets
115 g/4 oz fat bacon
1 clove garlic, crushed
4 eggs
280 ml/½ pint/1¼ cups thick Béchamel sauce (page 78)
12 rashers/slices of streaky bacon
salt and pepper to taste

Mince/grind the liver, anchovy fillets and fat bacon finely. Put the mixture in a blender and process. Mix in the crushed garlic, eggs and Béchamel. Season to taste. Line a shallow ovenproof dish with the streaky bacon and fill with the liver mixture. Place in a dish of cold water, cover and bake in a slow oven (150°C/300°F/gas 2) for 2 hours. When cooked, cover with greaseproof/waxed paper and press down with a weight. Leave for 24 hours in a cold place before serving with a salad vinaigrette.

NEWBAY BROWN BREAD

450 g/1 lb/4 cups coarse wholemeal flour
225 g/½ lb/2 cups pinhead oats
70 g/2½ oz/½ cup wheatgerm
70 g/2½ oz/½ cup wheat bran
70 g/2½ oz/5 tbsp plain flour
70 g/2½ oz/½ cup flake oatmeal
1 dsp/1½ US tbsp soft dark sugar
2 heaped and 1 flat tsp/2½ and 1¼ US tsp bread/baking soda
1 L/2 pints/5 cups buttermilk (room temperature)

Pre-heat oven to 230°C/450°F/gas 8. Grease 2 x 2 lb (1 kg) and 1 x 1 lb (½ kg) loaf tins well and dust with wheatgerm. Mix all the dry ingredients and add buttermilk to make a wet dough. Fill the tins, sprinkle with more wheatgerm and pat down. Put in the hot oven for 10 minutes. Then reduce heat (so as not to burn the outside of the bread) to 130°C/250°F/gas ½ and cook for 1 hour.

OISEAUX SANS TÊTES

Serves 6

Here is our own version of a German dish called *rouladen*. It looks like little birds when cooked and was given its title – birds without heads – by a Belgian guest.

round steak – 6 thin pieces around 140 g/5 oz each (ask butcher to slice it)
French mustard
Brussels pâté
6 smoked rindless rashers/slices of bacon
salt and pepper
1 onion, chopped
½ red pepper, chopped
olive oil

Take the thinly-sliced pieces of round steak and flatten them out to about 10-12 cm/4-5" square by placing them in a plastic bag and hitting them with a steak hammer or rolling pin. Rub on some French mustard. Place a thin slice of pâté on each, then a rasher/slice of bacon. Add salt and pepper. In olive oil, lightly sauté the onion and red pepper. When soft, remove from pan and spread over the meat. Roll up each piece of meat and tie with string. Sauté the steak parcels in olive oil and brown on all sides. Remove from pan very gently and lower into a heavy casserole and almost cover with water or beef stock. Braise over a very low heat for about 3 hours. Remove parcels carefully and keep warm. Strain and then thicken sauce with cornflour/corn starch and a glass of red wine, if desired. Remove string before serving with mashed potato and grated nutmeg. Can be made a day or two beforehand and reheated.

The splendidly-elegant Newport House is a country mansion overlooking the river and quay in Newport, County Mayo. For 200 years it was the country estate of the O'Donel family, descended from the fighting Earls of Tyrconnell who were transplanted from Ulster to Mayo by Oliver Cromwell. In 1945, the house and its fishery were bought by the late Henry Mumford-Smith, a renowned English angler, from the Irish-American owner who had himself purchased the property from the widow of Captain O'Donel. Newport then took on a new life as a country house hotel. The restoration was continued by Henry's son, the late Francis Mumford-Smith, and his wife Eleanor. In 1985, the estate was bought by Kieran and Thelma Thompson, who have maintained the traditions of the house and its friendly staff as well as carrying out extensive refurbishments.

Chef: John Gavin

SCALLOPS WITH CREAMED LEEK IN NOILLY PRAT SAUCE

Serves 2

8 scallops
225 g/8 oz leeks
60 ml/2 fl oz/¼ cup dry white wine
60 ml/2 fl oz/¼ cup water
115 ml/4 fl oz/½ cup cream
salt, pepper, nutmeg, fresh dill
55 g/2 oz/½ stick butter

Wash the leeks and cut into julienne strips. Cook in the white wine and water for 3 minutes. Add cream and reduce until thick. Season the scallops and quickly sauté in butter until golden brown.

Noilly Prat Sauce
60 ml/2 fl oz/¼ cup Noilly Prat
30 ml/1 fl oz/⅛ cup white wine
115 ml/4 fl oz/½ cup fish stock
15 g/½ oz/1 US tbsp shallots, finely chopped
115 ml/4 fl oz/½ cup cream
45 g/1½ oz/⅓ stick butter (to finish)
salt and pepper

to garnish: *fresh dill*

In a pan, reduce Noilly Prat, white wine, fish stock and chopped shallots by half. Add cream and reduce to the desired consistency. Pass through a fine sieve and swirl in the butter. Place 1" metal cutter on a plate. Fill with creamed leeks. Glaze under grill/broiler. Remove cutter and place scallops alongside glazed leeks. Coat with Noilly Prat sauce and garnish with a sprig of fresh dill.

Sauté Duck Breasts with Orange and Damson Sauce

4 duck breasts (140-170 g/5-6 oz each)
salt and pepper
55 g/2 oz/½ stick butter, preferably clarified
1 tbsp/1¼ US tbsp olive oil

♣

Season duck breasts with salt and pepper. Place butter and olive oil in heated frying pan. Add duck breasts. Sauté for 5 minutes on each side until pink. Allow to rest before serving with orange and damson sauce.

Orange and Damson Sauce
115 g/4 oz/½ cup caster sugar
60 ml/2 fl oz/¼ cup water
60 ml/2 fl oz/¼ cup vinegar (preferably tarragon)
140 ml/5 fl oz/⅔ cup orange juice
115 ml/4 fl oz/½ cup duck stock
115 g/4 oz fresh damsons, stones removed
salt and pepper to taste

to garnish: *orange segments, sprigs of basil*

♣

Caramelise sugar, water and vinegar. Add the orange juice. Simmer for 2 minutes until dissolved. Add duck stock and damsons and simmer for 5-7 minutes. Season with salt and pepper. (Thicken slightly with cornflour/corn starch if needed.) Garnish with orange segments and a sprig of basil.

Rhubarb Sorbet

340 g/¾ lb rhubarb
85 g/3 oz/3 tbsp caster sugar
30 ml/1 oz/⅛ cup water
juice of ¼ lemon

to garnish: *fresh mint*

♣

Using a thin rhubarb near root, wash, trim, peel and cut into 5 mm/ ¼" pieces. Place water in a saucepan, add rhubarb, sugar and lemon juice. Cover with lid and boil for 2 minutes. Remove lid and simmer for 7 minutes until cooked. Remove from heat and allow to cool, then purée and place in ice cream machine for 10-15 minutes. Store in freezer until needed.

To serve, mould the sorbet into oval shapes using 2 tablespoons dipped in hot water. Place 3 shapes in the centre of each chilled plate. Garnish with a sprig of mint.

BREAD AND BUTTER PUDDING WITH WHISKEY SAUCE

Pudding
12 slices white bread, toasted (cut 2 round shapes per slice)
55 g/2 oz/½ stick butter
55 g/2 oz/½ cup sultanas/raisins
2 whole eggs
85 g/3 oz/3 tbsp caster sugar
280 ml/½ pint/1¼ cups milk
280 ml/½ pint/1¼ cups cream
1 tbsp/1¼ US tbsp vanilla essence

Cut toast with 2" round cutter. Butter hot toast and place 1 round in the bottom of 4 small lightly-greased ramekin dishes. Add a layer of washed sultanas, and another slice of toast, building to approximately 2-3 layers in each ramekin. Whisk eggs and sugar. Add milk, cream and vanilla and pass through a fine strainer into a jug. Divide the mixture between each ramekin. Stand in a roasting tin half-full of water and cook in a moderate oven (150°C/300°F/gas 2) for ¾-1 hour.

Whiskey Sauce
140 g/5 oz/1¼ stick butter
115 g/4 oz/½ cup caster sugar
1 whole egg, beaten
1½ measures of Irish whiskey

Melt butter in a small saucepan, then add sugar. When sugar is dissolved, add beaten egg, whisking vigorously. Finally add the whiskey. Serve hot immediately or keep warm in a *bain-marie**.

Bain-marie: a large deep tray filled with hot water into which dishes requiring slow cooking in the oven are placed; also used for keeping soups and sauces warm.

Built around 1830 and originally including the house next door, The Old Presbytery in Kinsale was bequeathed to the Catholic Church at the beginning of this century by a wealthy Englishwoman. Under the terms of the legacy, the house was to be for the sole use of Catholic curates in perpetuity. It remained in Church hands until the late 1970s after which special permission from the previous owner's family had to be obtained in order to sell it. Ken and Cathleen Buggy bought The Old Presbytery, at that stage occupied only by cats and fat pigeons, in 1982. Since then, it has become a comfortable family home and a thriving guesthouse business.

The Old Presbytery

Cork Street,
Kinsale,
Co. Cork.
Phone: (021) 772027

NETTLE AND DANDELION SOUP

250 g/9 oz young nettle leaves or nettle tops (if a little later in the year)
250 g/9 oz young dandelion leaves
1 medium onion, sliced
1 small leek, roughly chopped
1 stick celery, roughly chopped
1 medium-to-large potato (200-250 g/8 oz), diced
100 g/3-4 oz/1 stick butter
1¼-1¾ L/2-3 pints/4-6 cups chicken stock

♣

Wash the nettle and dandelion leaves. Soften the onions in the butter on a low-to-medium flame (do not brown). Add the diced potato and sauté for a minute or two (do not permit them to brown or let the butter burn). Add leek and celery, continue to sauté for another minute or two, stirring frequently. Add the nettle and dandelion leaves (reserving a few of the latter as a garnish). Stir in well and continue to cook. As leaves begin to wilt, add the stock and bring gently to the boil. Lower the heat and simmer for 20-25 minutes.

Either liquidise the contents of the pot in a food processor or put them through a moulinette. Return the soup to the heat and season to taste (plenty of freshly-ground black pepper gives an added zest).

For garnish, roll the reserved dandelion leaves into tubes and slice thinly across to make a julienne to be sprinkled over the soup before serving.

This soup benefits from the addition of cream (1 or 2 tablespoons, depending on taste and size of helping). Add cream at last minute and do not stir.

Ken Buggy

'BEAN CAOIN' COD IN CREAM

This is a very old Irish dish with origins in Waterford.
Bean caoin (pronounced 'ban queen') means 'gentle woman' in Irish, the
equivalent of the French *bonne femme.*

900 g/2 lb cod fillets
450 g/1 lb/3 cups onions, sliced
2 medium carrots, sliced very, very thinly
140 g/5 oz/1¼ sticks butter
100 ml/4 fl oz/½ cup cream
salt and pepper
parsley, chopped
2 tsp/2½ US tsp paprika
pinch of cayenne (optional)

to serve: *parsley sprigs and lemon wedges*

♣

Pre-heat a flameproof casserole dish. Sweat the onions in the butter, add
the carrots – do not allow them to brown or overcook. Place the seasoned
fish on top of the vegetables. Add the cream, parsley and the paprika (and
cayenne if required). Bake at 180°C/350°F/gas 4 for 20-30 minutes, until
tender, but do not allow fish to overcook. Serve with a large bunch of
parsley and large lemon wedges (not slices).

IRISH COCKLE AND MUSSEL LOAF

175 g/6 oz cooked mussels
175 g/6 oz cooked cockles
280 ml/½ pint/1¼ cups good white wine fish stock
15 g/½ oz/2 tbsp gelatine, moistened in 4 tbsp/5 US tbsp dry white vermouth
280 ml/½ pint/1¼ cups chilled cream, beaten lightly
salt and pepper

♣

Bring fish stock to a gentle boil, then remove from heat. Stir in the softened gelatine and allow to cool. Mash or liquidise the mussels, cockles, gelatine mix and fish stock to form a rough consistency. Check seasoning. Fold the cream into the fish mixture and pour into an oiled mould. Cover with greaseproof/waxed paper and refrigerate for 2-3 hours (longer will not hurt). When ready to serve, turn pâté (actually a mousseline) onto a plate and decorate if desired.

Variation – before liquidising fish, boil 225 g/½ lb diced mushrooms slowly for 5 minutes in half the fish stock. Strain, set mushrooms aside and return liquid to saucepan in which gelatine, vermouth/fish-stock mix is to be prepared. Proceed as above, but stir mushrooms in when folding mixture. Once refrigerated, stir occasionally until almost set (this prevents the mushrooms from settling at the bottom).

An early Norman tower situated on the shores of Galway Bay, Oranmore Castle is now the home of the artist Leonie King and her husband Alec Finn, musician with the group De Danaan. The last family to live in the castle were the Blakes who, in the 1880s, demolished the adjoining Elizabethan buildings. Derelict for a hundred years, it was bought in the 1940s by Leonie's late mother, the writer Anita Leslie, for £150. Improvements have been made ever since, the latest addition being a solar-heated conservatory.

Oranmore Castle ~
Co GALWAY

JERUSALEM ARTICHOKE SOUP

5 large Jerusalem artichokes (roots)
1 onion, sliced
3 cloves of garlic, chopped
2 potatoes, diced
570 ml/1 pint/2½ cups light stock
570 ml/1 pint/2½ cups thick chicken stock
chives, chopped

Wash the artichokes and scrape skin off bulbous parts. Place them in a pot with the onion, garlic, potatoes and light stock. Boil gently until the vegetables are soft. Then add the thick chicken stock and boil again. Remove from the heat and put through a blender/food processor, adding salt and pepper to taste and some chopped chives.

ORANMORE MUSSELS

2 kg/4-5 lb mussels
2 slices streaky bacon (green, not smoked), chopped
4 tbsp/5 US tbsp olive oil or 60 g/2½ oz/¾ stick butter
1 large onion, chopped reasonably well
2 shallots/scallions, finely chopped
1-3 large cloves garlic (depending on enthusiasm), finely chopped
1 stick of fennel (or any one of the following: 1 tbsp fennel seeds,
2 star anise, 4 tbsp of any pastis)
2 tomatoes, peeled and roughly chopped
2 generous glasses white wine
salt and pepper

♣

Wash, scrape and beard the mussels. In a deep saucepan on a moderate heat, sweat the bacon in the oil or butter until the fat runs, but do not allow to crisp. Then add the onions, shallots or scallions and garlic and stick of fennel or the fennel seeds (neither of the others; if used see below) and cook gently until the onions are translucent. Do not allow to brown. Add the tomatoes and continue to cook, covered, until tomatoes are almost a purée. Do not salt because mussels can produce a great deal. Set aside and keep hot.

Put the wine into a large pot with (if either are used instead of fennel or seeds) the pastis or star anise. Cover and bring to the boil for about 1 minute. Add mussels and continue to boil for about 3 minutes. Remove opened mussels to a large heated bowl, discarding those which have failed to open. Strain mussel liquor, add it to the onion, bacon and tomato mix. Reheat if necessary, check seasoning and pour over mussels. Serve with lots of crusty bread.

LAMB'S LIVER WITH YOGURT AND MUSTARD

570 g/ 1¼ lb lamb's liver, sliced thinly
1 tsp/ 1½ US tsp grated horseradish
4 tsp/5 US tsp granular mustard
280 ml/½ pint/ 1 cup yogurt
4 rashers/slices smoked streaky bacon
3 scallions or 1 small onion, sliced thinly
1 clove garlic, chopped
4 tbsp/5 US tbsp cream
2 tbsp/2½ US tbsp Dry Martini
12 pickled nasturtium seeds (or capers)

to serve: *mashed potatoes with grated nutmeg*

Marinate the lamb's liver in the horseradish, mustard and yogurt. Fry bacon, then add the scallions or onions and garlic and cook over a medium heat until brown. Remove from the pan and set aside. Remove the liver from the marinade and pat dry. Add about 2-3 tbsp/3-4 US tbsp oil to the pan and turn up the heat. When hot, add liver and fry each slice quickly on both sides. Remove from the pan with a slotted spoon. Return the bacon-onion mixture and the remains of the marinade to the pan. Stir in cream, Martini and nasturtium seeds. Add the liver to warm through, then transfer everything to a heated dish. Serve with mashed potatoes topped with a little grated nutmeg.

Partry House was built in 1667 as a dower house to nearby Castle Carra, on the shores of Lough Carra in County Mayo. Set in 250 acres of land, it is now the home of film makers David Shaw-Smith and his wife, Sally-Ann, who have made over forty films on traditional crafts.

PARTRY PIKE

Partry House lies on the shores of beautiful Lough Carra. This tranquil lake
holds many fine trout as well as the ubiquitous pike. Though despised by
many, the flesh of the pike is firm and white and takes well to strong
aromatic flavourings.

*1 pike, 1¾-2¾ kg/4-6 lb (This may seem large for four people, but this is the
best size for cooking. Any smaller and the bones are a problem;
much larger and it will be too coarse.)
2 bunches of spring onions
piece of fresh ginger, approximately 5 cm x 2½ cm/2" x 1"
garlic, at least 10 cloves
1 lemon, peeled and squeezed
large carton fromage blanc or crème fraîche (Jockey)
salt and freshly-ground black pepper*

Place the whole (but gutted) pike in a fish kettle or pan large enough to
hold it comfortably. Cover with cold, salted water and bring slowly to the
boil. Remove immediately from the heat and allow the pike to cool in the
water. Trim the spring onions. Set 4 or 5 aside and place the rest in a food
processor with the peeled ginger and garlic cloves. Process to a stiff paste.
This has the most wonderful fresh pungent smell. Add the lemon juice and
enough of the fish liquid to make it slightly liquid. Process again. Pour into
a small saucepan and simmer gently for about 5 minutes. Strain, pressing
hard with a wooden spoon to extract every drop of liquid.

Recipe continued over

Sally Ann Shaw-Smith.

When cool, lift the pike out of the pan carefully. Remove the head and tail and the skin on the upper side. Gently ease the top fillets off onto a large plate. Carefully pull out the backbone and any loose bones. Turn the fish over and remove the rest of the skin. Arrange the rest of the fish on the serving dish. Keep covered in a warm place. Blanch the lemon peel and make julienne strips. Finely slice the remaining spring onions. Whisk the spring onion/garlic/ginger liquid into the fromage blanc. Reheat gently and pour over the fish. Sprinkle with the sliced spring onions and fine julienne lemon rind and serve immediately. It is absolutely delicious accompanied by brown rice and broccoli.

ROAST LEG OF LAMB

Here in the west of Ireland, with the Maumtrasna Mountains across the lake, the lamb is particularly delicious. It needs nothing more than lashings of fragrant pink garlic, golden baked potatoes, lightly steamed asparagus and a great bunch of aromatic mint – all straight from our own walled garden – to make a feast fit for a bishop!

1½-2 kg/3-4 lb leg of lamb
suet to cover
loads of garlic
a little extra-virgin olive oil

With a slim, sharp knife, make incisions just under the skin of the leg of lamb and stuff with as many peeled and crushed garlic cloves as you can squeeze in. Pour a little of the oil into a roasting dish, place the lamb in it and cover completely with an opened-out piece of suet (this keeps the meat moist and tender and automatically bastes it). Cook in a moderately hot oven (230°C/450°F/gas 8) for 1¼ hours. (I use the top right-hand oven in a 4-door Aga.) After about 50 minutes, remove the suet covering and allow to brown for the remaining time. Allow the roast to rest for at least 20 minutes before carving.

To make the gravy
Pour almost all the fat out of the roasting pan. Add a sprinkling of flour, sea salt and freshly-ground black pepper to the juices in the pan and cook for a couple of minutes. Gradually add the water over which the vegetables suggested above have been steamed until it is of the right consistency. Cook for another couple of minutes. Pour into a heated gravy jug and serve with the roast.

BLACKBERRY BOMBE

In the autumn, the lanes around Partry are laden with fat, juicy blackberries
crying out to be picked. They are so sweet they need hardly any additional
sugar. Blackberry tart and blackberry crumble are both good old favourites,
but this pudding is really something special!

900 g/2 lb ripe blackberries
55 g/2 oz/2 tbsp caster sugar
½ oz/2 tbsp gelatine (powdered) per pint/2½ US cups of purée
280 ml/½ pint/1¼ cups double cream
dash of caster sugar

Meringues
4 egg whites
225 g/8 oz/1 cup caster sugar
pinch of salt
¼ tsp cochineal

Make the meringues beforehand and store in an airtight tin. Beat the egg
whites with the salt until stiff, then gradually whisk in the caster sugar. Fold
in the colouring. Pipe or spoon 20p/50¢ size meringues onto sheets of
nonstick greaseproof/waxed paper. Bake very, very slowly in bottom left-
hand oven in 4-door Aga, preferably overnight, until firm and dry, or at
110°C/225°F/gas ¼ for at least 2½ hours and then turn upside-down to dry
out.

Place blackberries in a covered pan and heat gently until the juices
start to run and the berries are just soft. Add the caster sugar and stir until
dissolved. Purée the fruit and then sieve to remove all the seeds. Measure
the purée and sprinkle the appropriate amount of gelatine onto 3 tbsp/
3¾ US tbsp cold water in a small saucepan. Heat slowly, stirring all the time
until completely dissolved. Fold well into the purée and pour into a cold
bowl. Allow to set overnight.

When ready to serve, dip the bowl into a basin of hot water for a
couple of seconds and then turn out onto a large serving dish. Cover with
the cream, stiffly beaten with the dash of caster sugar, and stud all over with
the small rich-pink meringues. Serve with plain unwhipped cream. This
pudding looks simply wonderful on a large oval dish decorated with sprays
of autumn brambles.

Everything that surrounds the ebullient Irish potter Stephen Pearce reflects a
confident philosophy of design inherited from his late parents, his mother Lucy and
his father, the potter Philip Pearce. His spacious house, built beside his studio in the
1970s to his own plans, is a combination of stone, wood and slate and is filled with
light. Its interior fittings and furnishings were also made to his own specifications.
The recent addition of a tower was influenced by New England house and barn
styles. Stephen's mother was a gifted cook. She passed a love of good food on to her
son, which continues to inspire the beautiful tableware he creates.

THREE SOUPS

If you are the sort of person who boils chicken bones for stock, then here
are three of my own soups. Reduce stock so that it is not watery,
not too strong.

570 ml/1 pint/2½ cups stock
1 or 2 leeks, or spring cabbage, or fresh broccoli
2 or 3 slices of fresh ginger
2 cloves garlic
black pepper, freshly ground
salt
1 tsp/1¼ US tsp honey

♣

Bring stock to the boil, add peeled cloves of garlic and slices of ginger and
the chosen vegetable. Boil for 5 to 10 minutes (according to how crunchy
you like your veg). Add salt, pepper and honey to taste. Serve immediately.

Every dish is a matter of personal taste. In creating these three soups, I
have simply adapted the Chinese technique of poaching fresh ingredients in
chicken stock, with an instant infusion of garlic and ginger, so you end up
with crisp vegetables and a hint of garlic and ginger. It is as quick to make
as instant soup and infinitely variable. Keep your jug of chicken stock in the
fridge.

Stephen Pearce.

BLACK PUDDING AND SWEET APPLES

I once had this in a bar in Lyon with a bottle of crisp Beaujolais. The black pudding must be genuine and without grains. It is simply blood, chunks of crisp pork belly fat and the correct condiments in a natural skin casing.

♣

Cut the ring of pudding in half. Then split each half lengthways and fry in butter on both sides, not for too long. Take 2 eating apples (cooking apples work just as well), cut into segments, peel and core. Fry them in honey and butter. You will be surprised at how much honey you can use. This will take 10-15 minutes on a slow heat.

CRISPALEENY SPUDS

This is from Kim-Mai's family. I like it on a Friday evening as it takes just over an hour to cook. So if I prepare a salad and don't dress it, leave a sirloin steak and some freshly-made English mustard, I have time for two pints of Murphy's stout while the crispaleenies are cooking. Then I return to cook the steak by the method Michael Ryan learned in the three-star kitchens of France. After a night of tasting rich sauces, all the chefs want is a piece of real meat, so heat up a pan very hot, throw on a handful of sea salt and small fistful of fresh thyme. Lay down the steak and let each side cook for less than 2 minutes. My variation is to sit the fat end on the pan for 3 minutes so I can eat the crispy fat with the blue meat.

♣

Oh yes, the crispaleenies. Peel some medium-size spuds and steam for 5 minutes. Heat some olive oil and 2 cloves of garlic in a baking tray. Cut spuds in half and score the roundy side every quarter of an inch, toss with a little salt in olive oil. Then put the tray in a hot oven for an hour.

For a special treat, I have a pot of goose fat which is even better than olive oil for crispaleenies.

BACON AND POTATO PIE

This hearty dish comes from my Welsh grandmother. It is wonderful when washed down with a bottle of robust red Burgundy. The quantities given are a guideline and adjustable to taste.

8 medium potatoes
450 g/1 lb streaky rashers/slices of bacon
2 medium onions
2 cloves garlic
½ cup olive oil
salt and pepper
3 tomatoes
a little thyme

♣

I have made this in one of my own dishes for twenty years, though I've managed never to have to wash the pot. Use a cast iron pot or thick-bottomed casserole.

Peel potatoes and onions and slice thinly. Take rinds off rashers and cut into 2½ cm/1" pieces. Slice tomatoes and crush garlic.

Put a little olive oil in the bottom of the pot. Now, a layer of potatoes, then a layer of bacon, then a few onion rings. Repeat this about 4 times, each time putting a little olive oil over the onion. For the final 3 or 4 layers, put tomato on top of the onion, plus a little thyme and garlic, salt and pepper and olive oil. The flavours from the top layers will travel down during cooking, so if you decide to put salt or garlic low down in the mix, the bottom may become too salty or garlicky. Olive oil is to taste; I use a lot. My sweetheart Kim-Mai uses much less oil and a little butter on top.

Bill Hogan in Schull makes a cheese called Gabriel which melts and gets crisp and gooey, like a superior Gruyére. A good shot of this in small chunks (or grated Parmesan) put on top 20 minutes before the end of cooking is a great variation. Cooking time is ¾-1 hour at 200°C/400°F/gas 6. Cover the pot during cooking, but remove for last 20 minutes to crisp.

One of Ireland's finest Palladian buildings and the last great intact eighteenth-
century mansion in County Roscommon, Strokestown Park House was once a
30,000 acre estate on which the lives of tens of thousands of local people depended.
It was built for Thomas Mahon MP during the 1730s by the noted German architect
Richard Castle. The galleried kitchen which he designed in the south wing allowed
the lady of the house to drop the menus down every Monday morning with
instructions for the week's meals. In 1979, Strokestown, then dwindled to 300 acres,
was bought by a local firm, Westward Garages. Since then, the house and gardens
have been restored and opened to the public under the administration of
Luke Dodd. The restoration includes the opening of Ireland's first museum devoted
to the Famine of the 1840s.

STROKESTOWN PARK HOUSE

STROKESTOWN POTATO FRITTERS

This is a fancy Boxty, a traditional Irish dish made with potatoes.

1 small-medium onion, chopped finely
1 large egg
1 heaped tbsp/1½ US tbsp cornflour/corn starch
3 large potatoes, peeled and grated
vegetable oil
½ tsp salt

Combine the onion, egg, salt and cornflour/corn starch. Grate the potato only when ready to cook the fritters as it will blacken and look a bit distasteful. Heat 6-8 tablespoons of oil in a pan. When hot, spoon individual tablespoonsful of the mixture into the pan and flatten out. Cook on one side and then turn over. They take about 3-4 minutes each side and turn a wonderful golden colour. For a more spicy version, a few cumin seeds can be added to the mixture. These are particularly good served with steak. They are also good for breakfast served with the traditional fry or on their own with apple sauce and sour cream.

County Roscommon, Ireland. Telephone 078–33013

STROKESTOWN PARK POTATO PUDDING

This has been adapted from an eighteenth-century recipe.

Shortcrust Pastry
225 g/8 oz/2 cups plain flour
115 g/4 oz/1 stick butter
1 egg, beaten

Filling
340 g/¾ lb potatoes (Pinks or Golden Wonders)
225 g/8 oz/2 sticks butter
450 g/1 lb/2¼ cups caster sugar
8 egg yolks (free range)
rind of 1 lemon
juice of ½ lemon
30 g/1 oz/¼ cup candied peel (home-made)
3 tbsp/3¾ US tbsp brandy

To make pastry, rub butter into flour and bind with beaten egg. Refrigerate for at least 1 hour before use.

Scrub potatoes and boil in their jackets until cooked. Remove skins and mash thoroughly or blend in a food processor. Cream the butter and sugar. Gradually add the egg yolks. Add the lemon rind, juice, the candied peel (chopped very finely) and the brandy. Finally, add the mashed potato and mix thoroughly.

Grease a 25 cm/11" diameter, 4 cm/1.5" deep tin with removable bottom with butter and line with the pastry. Pour the filling into the case and bake in a moderate oven (180°C/350°F/gas 4) for about 1 hour. Don't worry if the filling appears very wobbly when removed from the oven as it will set when the pudding cools down, although the centre will have the consistency of a mature soft cheese. Serve chilled with cream piped around the diameter. The pudding has a distinct flavour of almonds and a small slice is enough!

CATHERINE'S SCONES

900 g/2 lb/8 cups plain flour
3½ tsp/4½ US tsp (heaped) baking powder
200 g/7 oz/scant 2 sticks butter
2 tbsp/2½ US tbsp sugar
pinch of salt
225 g/8 oz/1½ cups sultanas/raisins
4 large eggs, beaten
500 ml/16 fl oz/2 cups milk

♣

Sift flour and baking powder. Rub in the butter; if using a food processor, make sure the butter is hard. Add the sugar and fruit and mix well. Beat the eggs and mix with the milk. Make a well in the centre of the dry ingredients. Pour in almost all the liquid (reserving some as a wash) and mix with a large metal fork. The mixture will be quite wet. Turn out on a floured surface and flatten with the hands to about 2 cm/¾". Cut the scones out and shape with the hands. Bake on a greased and floured baking tray in a moderate oven (180°C/350°F/gas 4) for approximately 30 minutes. Cool on a wire tray.

ELDERBERRY AND APPLE JELLY

First, collect large quantities of elderberries and apples. For the apples, any sort will do. If you can locate some crabs, these would be ideal; if not, windfalls are just as good.

Clean the apples and remove any damaged bits (use a stainless steel knife only). Cut up roughly. Fill your largest stainless steel pan with apples and cover with water. Boil until the apples have completely disintegrated. Flavourings such as clove, orange, lemon etc. can be added during this process. Strain the resultant liquid through muslin (this may be done overnight as it is a fairly lengthy process).

Collect elderberries on the twig. Fill your largest stainless steel pan with the berries and cover with water. Boil until the fruit has yielded all the juice (at least 1 hour). Strain as above.

Combine 570 ml/1 pint/2½ cups of the apple 'juice' to 1.1 L/2 pints/ 5 cups of the elderberry juice. Bring to the boil in a stainless steel pan. Heat 1.35 kg/3 lb/6¾ cups of sugar and combine with juices. Make sure the sugar is dissolved before bringing the mixture back to the boil. Continue to boil until the jelly sets on cooled plates. Bottle in sterilised jars and seal in the normal way. Three pints of juice should yield about seven 1 lb-pots of jelly.

Tullanisk was built around 1795 for Sir Lawrence Parsons, afterwards 2nd Earl of Rosse, as a dower house for Birr Castle, although it was never used as such. Two younger brothers lived here during the middle of the last century and rumour has it that they didn't see eye to eye, so many rooms are duplicated. A rectangular classical house with four formal fronts, Tullanisk is notable for its enormous tripartite window on the first floor directly over the fanlighted front door. Until her death, it was for many years the home of Mariga Guinness of the Irish Georgian Society. George and Susan Gossip and their family came here in the winter of 1989 and opened Tullanisk to guests in September 1990.

CLONBROCK BREAKFAST SCONES

This recipe, a version of griddle bread, is said to have been obtained by Susie's great-great-grandfather, Robert Dillon, 3rd Lord Clonbrock, who was given scones like these when sailing around the Aran Islands in the late 1830s. They were a frequent dish at Clonbrock, her family home in County Galway. We were given the recipe by her mother, Audrey Dillon-Mahon.

225 g/8 oz/2 cups wholemeal flour (we use Abbey Stoneground)
55 g/2 oz/½ stick butter
pinch of salt
buttermilk

♣

Rub butter into flour and salt. Mix with buttermilk to a soft dough. Roll out to a rectangle, 1 cm/½" thick. Cut into 8 rectangular portions. (If you try to make more, they will be too thin.) To cook, slowly heat a griddle or frying pan, lightly greased with butter, to a high heat. Fry the scones and turn when brown. When ready, they should be brown on the outside and soft, almost raw, inside. Serve immediately with butter and jam, honey or marmalade.

CHICKEN WITH MORELS

We are lucky enough to find morels growing wild in the woods at Tullanisk
each spring. We usually pick enough to make this delicious recipe at
least once.

2 medium-sized chickens
450 g/1 lb fresh morels or 55 g/2 oz dried morels*
2 generous glasses dry white wine
280 ml/½ pint/1¼ cups cream
1 tsp/1¼ US tsp green peppercorns
generous bunch chives, chopped
salt and pepper

♣

If you have fresh morels (see note * below), cut them in half from top to
bottom and soak for 5 minutes in salted water to remove slugs or insects.
Drain carefully and pat dry. If using other mushrooms, wipe them clean with
a slightly damp cloth, using the point of a knife to clear out bits of leaf and
any obvious insects. If using dried morels or other dried mushrooms, put
them in a bowl with just enough warm water barely to cover them. Leave for
a least 1 hour (up to 4 or 5 will do no harm), checking occasionally to see
that they have absorbed the water and do not need a little more.

Using a heavy-bottomed pan, bring 1 glass of white wine to the
simmer and stew the morels gently for 10 minutes. Set aside to cool.

Bone one of the chickens (if you have a friendly butcher, ask him to
do it for you). With a sharp knife, remove all the flesh from the breast and
legs of the second chicken. Carefully remove as much fat and skin as
possible. Chop into large bite-sized pieces.

Slice 4 of the largest cooked morel halves into thin slices (if using
dried mushrooms, this is about 125 g/4 oz, wet weight). Mix them well with
the chicken pieces and season. Stuff the boned chicken with this mixture
and sew up carefully. Roast in a moderate oven (190°C/375°F/gas 4-5) for
about 1¼ hours or until done. Remove from roasting pan and keep warm.

Leave the pan juices (with the aid of a bulb baster or spoon, remove
any obvious surplus fat), add a second generous glass of wine and bring to
the boil. Add green peppercorns immediately, then the morels and all their
juices. Add cream and boil down rapidly until thick. Check the seasoning
and add the chopped chives.

Slice the chicken into thick slices. Either put them into a deep,
warmed serving dish and cover with the morel sauce, or serve the sauce in
a separate bowl, but be sure to share the morels!

Any leftovers can be reheated in the sauce. This dish can also be prepared in advance and gently reheated. An acceptable alternative is plainly-roasted chicken with the morel sauce – quite good, but not nearly as good as the above.

* Morels, if you can find them, are in season in the late spring. They can be bought but are outrageously expensive. Dried morels can also be bought, but they too are expensive. This dish is very good with any of the more highly-flavoured woodland mushrooms, for example ceps, chanterelles, horn of plenty, wood-hedgehog or blewits, all of which grow freely in Ireland from about July until November. Some, like fresh chanterelles and blewits, are even sold cheaply in certain up-market supermarkets. All can be bought dried. If using dried ceps, split the quantity with something a little less overpowering. Field mushrooms will not work with this recipe as they are too mild in taste.

GAME PIE

This is an ideal way to use up old or damaged pheasants and the odd pigeon or the like for which you cannot think up a good use. It is really delicious and none the worse for this. Do try to use a number of different types of game for this as it dramatically improves the flavour. Hare is especially good but on no account use duck.

680 g/1½ lb game meat, off the bone and sliced or diced
(pheasant, pigeon, hare, venison)
225 g/8 oz streaky bacon (not rashers), diced
140 ml/¼ pint/⅔ cup game stock
(made from the bones of a hare for preference)
140 ml/¼ pint/⅔ cup red wine
225 g/8 oz button mushrooms
225 g/8 oz pickling onions (or sliced large onions)
2 cloves garlic, chopped
salt and pepper
bay leaf
seasoned flour
butter and oil
340 g/12 oz puff pastry
1 egg
milk

♣

Fry onions lightly in butter until golden. Add chopped garlic and fry for a further minute. Sprinkle meats with seasoned flour and brown gently in a little oil. Stew slowly in a heavy saucepan (covered) with onions, garlic, bay leaf, stock and wine. Just before meat is done, add mushrooms and continue cooking until everything is tender. If there is too much sauce, strain and return the sauce to the heat and boil down rapidly until sufficiently reduced. Allow to cool. (This stage is best completed a day or so in advance for the flavours to intensify. It may also be made up in larger amounts and frozen in the required portions.)

Line a small pie dish with puff pastry, fill with the mixture (having first checked the seasoning). Cover, decorate and glaze with an egg wash. Bake in a hot oven (230°C/450°F/gas 8) until golden brown. Serve with baked or mashed potatoes, red cabbage, celery and redcurrant jelly.

♣

Index